April 30, 2006

Much Love to Our sister
Clavetta

You will be well soon

Gheetha & John

LIFE'S LITTLE PRAYER BOOK

COMPILED BY GARY LAHODA

TESTAMENT
BOOKS

New York

This 2000 edition is published by Testament Books™, an imprint of
Random House Value Publishing, Inc., 280 Park Avenue, New York, NY 10017,
by arrangement with Ottenheimer Publishers, Inc.
5 Park Center Court, Suite 300, Owings Mills, MD 21117.

Testament Books™ and design are trademarks
of Random House Value Publishing, Inc.

Random House
New York • Toronto • London • Sydney • Auckland
http://www.randomhouse.com/

Printed and bound in the United States of America.

A catalog record for this title is available from the Library of Congress.

ISBN: 0-517-16198-2

9 8 7 6 5 4 3 2 1

For most of us, fulfilment in life lies seemingly just beyond our grasp. No matter how successful a life we lead, we'll admit, if pressed, that there is something missing.

Millions of us try to fill that gap by seeking a closer connection with God through prayer. We come from many walks of life. We have different needs, different hopes, different loves. This collection of prayers was assembled to reflect that diversity. Based on the Judeo-Christian tradition, they were chosen from the Bible and writings of saints, mystics, and contemporary authors.

Their main purpose is to provide inspiration: to nudge the reader into a frame of mind that will enhance the link we all have with the Almighty.

Saint Augustine, one of the earliest church fathers, said that "God loves each one of us, as if there were *only* one of us." These writers obviously believe that returning God's love, and loving each other, as well, is the best way to meet life's needs. And no matter how *well* we love, if the wise men of the past are right, we will win our reward.

∽ *Gary Lahoda* ∽

Prayer Number

~ 1 ~

May the God of peace . . . equip you
with everything good for doing his will. . . .

Hebrews 13:20 (NIV)*

*New International Version

~ 2 ~

I know, O Lord, that a man's life is not his own;
    it is not for man to direct his steps.
Correct me, Lord, but only with justice—
    not in your anger, lest you reduce me to nothing.

Jeremiah 10:23-24 (NIV)

~ 3 ~

Give me, O Lord, a steadfast heart,
    which no unworthy affection may drag downwards.
Give me an unconquered heart, which no tribulation can wear out.
Give me an upright heart, which no unworthy purpose may tempt aside.
Bestow upon me also, O Lord my God,
    understanding to know you, diligence to seek you,
    wisdom to find you, and a faithfulness
    that may finally embrace you. Amen.

St. Thomas Aquinas

~ 4 ~

Lord help me to live that others may
Be glad I chanced to pass their way.
Help me to smile through worry and care.
Teach me that burdens lighten through prayer.

May it never be said that I failed to lend
A helping hand to the need of a friend.
Grant that seeing Christ in others
I may recognize them as my brothers.

Most of all, let me live in thy grace
Content with my role in the human race;
That when this earthly life is through,
I may share eternity with you.

Eleanor Larson

~ 5 ~

O my divine Savior,
Thou art my book, my mirror.
I will consult thee always to learn what I must do.
I desire that thy actions be the rule of my actions.
Grant me this grace. . . .

Abbe Lasausse

~ 6 ~

O God, the Father of our Savior Jesus Christ . . .
    Sanctify, O Lord, our souls and bodies and spirits,
    search our consciences,
And cast out of us every evil thought, every base desire,
    all envy and pride,
    all wrath and anger, and all that is contrary to your holy will.
And grant us, O Lord . . . with a pure heart and contrite soul,
    to call upon you, our holy God and Father who is in heaven.

Liturgy of St. James

~ 7 ~

O God, grant that looking upon the face of the Lord,
    as into a glass, we may be changed into his likeness,
    from glory to glory.
Take out of us all pride and vanity, boasting and forwardness;
    and give us the true courage which shows itself by gentleness;
The true wisdom which shows itself by simplicity;
    and the true power which shows itself by modesty.

Charles Kingsley

~ 8 ~

Blessed are thou, O Lord our God, King of the universe,
    who makest the bands of sleep to fall upon mine eyes,
    and slumber upon mine eyelids.
May it be thy will, O Lord my God and God of my fathers,
    to suffer me to lie down in peace
    and to let me rise up again in peace.
Let not my thoughts trouble me, nor evil dreams, nor evil fancies,
    but let my rest be perfect before thee.
O lighten mine eyes, lest I sleep the sleep of death,
    for it is thou who givest light to the apple of the eye.
Blessed art thou, O Lord, who givest light to the whole world in
    thy glory.

Hebrew Prayer

~ 9 ~

Answer me quickly, O Lord;
    my spirit faints with longing. . . .
Let the morning bring me word of your unfailing love,
    for I have put my trust in you.
Show me the way I should go,
    for to you I lift up my soul.

Psalm 143:7–8 (NIV)

～ 10 ～

Today I promise I'll be true
    and do the things I ought to do.
I'll keep my thoughts all shining bright
    my spirits buoyant, clean and light.
I'll speak with calm and careful tongue;
    rejoice when I see work well done.
I'll love my neighbor down the street
    and guard my sometimes wayward feet.
I'll seek the best, the fine and true,
    and let no angry thoughts come through.
I'll offer help when need I see,
    for that's the way I ought to be.
And can I, Lord, this promise keep,
    and when at night lie down to sleep
Remember that my thanks are due—to God,
    the one who saw me through.

Mabel Warburton

～ 11 ～

O Lord, help us to be masters of ourselves,
that we may be servants of others.

Sir Alexander Paterson

~ *12* ~

May our Lord Jesus Christ himself and God our Father,
who loved us and by his grace
gave us eternal encouragement and good hope,
encourage your hearts and strengthen you
in every good deed and word.

II Thessalonians 2:16–17 (NIV)

~ *13* ~

Give me, dear Lord, thy conscious support
And let me be filled with the love and zeal
That give character and direction
To the activities of mind and body.

Myrtle Fillmore

~ *14* ~

May the grace of the Lord Jesus Christ, and the love of God,
and the fellowship of the Holy Spirit be with you all.

II Corinthians 13:14 (NIV)

~ 15 ~

O God the Holy Ghost, most loving Comforter of the fainthearted,
I beseech thee ever to turn that which is evil in me into good
And that which is good into that which is better.
Turn my mourning into joy,
My wandering feet into the right path,
My ignorance into knowledge of thy truth,
My lukewarmness into zeal, my fear into love,
All my material good into a spiritual gift,
All my earthly desires into heavenly,
All that is transient into that which lasts forever,
Everything human into that which is divine,
Everything created and finite into that sovereign
And immeasurable good, which thou thyself art,
O my God and Savior.

Thomas à Kempis

~ 16 ~

O Lord, I call to you; come quickly to me.
Hear my voice when I call to you.
Set a guard over my mouth, O Lord;
    keep watch over the door of my lips.
Let not my heart be drawn to what is evil,
    to take part in wicked deeds with men who are evildoers;
Let me not eat of their delicacies.

Psalm 141:1, 3-4 (NIV)

～ 17 ～

We give thanks unto you, heavenly Father,
 through Jesus Christ, your dear Son,
That you have this day so graciously protected us.
And we beg you to forgive us all our sins,
 and the wrong which we have done,
And by your great mercy defend us
 from all the perils and dangers of this night.
Into your hands we commend our bodies and souls,
 and all that is ours.
Let your holy angel have charge concerning us,
 that the wicked one have no power over us.

Martin Luther

～ 18 ～

Now I lay me down to sleep,
I pray thee, Lord, thy child to keep;
Thy love go with me all the night
And wake me with the morning light.

Author unknown

~ *19* ~

O God, we give you thanks for giving us each other—
For being together, which makes such a difference;
For having a good home, and for what we do there;
For games to play, and books and bikes and things to use;
For adventures to share, and dreams to dream of the future;
Save us from spoiling things—
By being conceited;
By being disobedient;
By being untrustworthy.
We want to get the very best out of each day that you give us—
Out of each job;
Out of each meal;
Out of each game;
Out of each friendship.
Show us how to do this in the way that Jesus did.
And for his sake.

Rita F. Snowden

~ *20* ~

May the God who gives endurance and encouragement
    give you a spirit of unity among yourselves
    as you follow Christ Jesus,
    so that with one heart and mouth you may glorify
    the God and Father of our Lord Jesus Christ.

Romans 15:5-6 (NIV)

～ 21 ～

Lord,
My family stands in need of a strength
    that is not in my power to give.
Even if I had it I could not give it.
I can feed them.
I can mend their jeans.
But I cannot give them the one thing they need most—
    that is a faith—a strength—to live by. . . .
I can lead them in what I feel to be right directions, Lord,
    and I can live before them the best way that I know how.
That's all that I can do—and it isn't enough.
Lord, God—give them strength.
Pursue them.
Grant them no peace until they find that peace is in thee.
Lure them into finding the faith
    that will help them stand steady in the world.

Jo Carr & Imogene Sorley

～ 22 ～

Give to us more faith.
We have so little . . . we say.
Yet we have faith in each other—in checks and banks,
    in trains and airplanes, in cooks,
    and in strangers who drive us in cabs.
Forgive us for our stupidity,
That we have faith in people whom we do not know,
And are reluctant to have faith in you who knows us altogether.

Peter Marshall

～ 23 ～

Today, Lord, give me courage, if indeed it is your Will,
To stand for all things righteous, all your desires fulfill.
In my weakness I may falter, extend your hand I pray.
I cannot walk alone, Dear Lord. Please guide my path today.
May I portray your goodness, so those I meet may see,
The wonder of your power, as your love shines through me.
And at the ending of this day I will thankfully behold,
How you and I together, Lord, achieved a worthy goal.
Amen.

Nancy Tant

～ 24 ～

Grant, O Lord, that we may carefully watch over our tempers
    and every unholy feeling.
Remove whatever in us may be a stumbling block in another's way.
That, by conforming to your will in small things,
    we may hope by your protection and help to pass safely
    through the greater dangers and trials
    to which we may be exposed.

Christina Rossetti

~ *25* ~

God of our fathers and our God,
Give us the faith to believe in the ultimate triumph of righteousness,
    no matter how dark and uncertain are the skies of today.
We pray for the bifocals of faith—that see the despair
    and the need of the hour
        but also see, further on, the patience of our God working out
        His plan in the world he has made.
Make our faith honest by helping us this day to do one thing
    because thou hast said, "Do it,"
Or to abstain because thou hast said, "Thou shalt not."
May our faith be seen in our works. Amen.

Peter Marshall

~ *26* ~

O Heavenly Father, in whom we live and move and have our being,
    we humbly pray you so to guide and govern us
    by your Holy Spirit,
That in all the cares and occupations of our daily life
    we may never forget you,
    but remember that we are ever walking in your sight.
For your name's sake.

Fifth Century Prayerbook

~ 27 ~

Dear Lord,
I give thanks for this little child, for her wide-eyed inquiry,
     for the openness with which she accepts others. . . .
Her path has crossed mine only for this short while, but knowing her
     has been one of those unexpected bonuses that life has to offer.
Ah, Lord, I have much to learn from her.
She chuckles often, for no other reason than her awareness
     that her world is good—that she is loved.
She loves others as naturally as flowers open to the sun. . . .
And she's curious, Lord, alive—awake to what is around her,
     and to the delightful possibilities of it all.
Ah, Lord—I give thanks for this little child.

Jo Carr & Imogene Sorley

~ 28 ~

Take full possession of my heart,
     raise there your throne,
     and command there as you do in heaven.
Being created by you, let me live to you.
Being created for you, let me act for your glory.
Being redeemed by you, let me render unto you what is yours,
     and let my spirit ever cleave to you alone.

John Wesley

~ 29 ~

Awake, my soul!
Awake, harp and lyre!
I will awaken the dawn.
I will praise you, O Lord, among the nations;
I will sing of you among the peoples.
For great is your love, reaching to the heavens;
     your faithfulness reaches to the skies.
Be exalted, O God, above the heavens;
     let your glory be over all the earth.

Psalm 57:8-11 (NIV)

~ 30 ~

Christ, our Savior, come thou to dwell within us,
That we may go forth with the light of thy hope in our eyes,
And thy faith and love in our hearts.

Gregorian Sacramentary

~ 31 ~

My God, I believe there is nothing better
     than to fulfil with joy, with love, thy will.
What wilt thou that I do?
I am ready.

Abbe Lasausse

~ *32* ~

We pray you, O Creator of everything, at this hour preceding night,
    that you be clement and watch over us.
Let dreams and phantoms of the night be scattered.
Keep us safe from our enemies and make us pure!

St. Ambrose

~ *33* ~

Bless all your people, the flocks of your fold.
Send down into our hearts the peace of heaven,
    and grant us also the peace of this life.
Give life to the souls of all of us,
    and let no deadly sin prevail against us, or any of your people.
Deliver all who are in trouble,
    for you are our God, who sets the captives free;
Who gives hope to the hopeless, and help to the helpless;
    who lifts up the fallen;
    and who is the haven of the shipwrecked.
Give your pity, pardon, and refreshment to every Christian soul,
    whether in affliction or error.
Preserve us, in our pilgrimage through this life,
    from hurt and danger,
    and grant that we may end our lives as Christians,
    well-pleasing to you,
And free from sin, and that we may have our portion and lot
    with all your saints.
For the sake of Jesus Christ our Lord and Savior.

Liturgy of St. Mark

~ *34* ~

In this agonizing crisis, Lord,
When my husband is jolted by the twisted turn of events
And everything seems to be wrong
I desperately long to help him.
I ache to break the intense pressure—
To lessen the hurt and confusion.
Yet all I can do is listen.
I can be a sounding board while he bounces back
Frustrations, fears, feelings.
I can be at his side when he comes home depleted.
I can *pray* what I can't possibly *say*
For deep within me I know the final decision
Has to be his.

Lord, that's not true:
The final decision has to be yours.

Ruth Harms Calkin

~ *35* ~

Show us, good Lord,
The peace we should seek
The peace we must give
The peace we can keep
The peace we must forgo,
And the peace you have given in Jesus our Lord.

from Contemporary Prayers for Public Worship

~ 36 ~

Lord,
I need to enlarge the place of my tent,
    and stretch out the curtains of my habitation;
For I have confined my love, my concern,
    within the four walls of my own household.
I minister sincerely to the needs of my family,
    but I manage to remain undisturbed by the needs of all others. . . .
Dear Lord, help me enlarge the place of my tent.
Help me reach beyond my own front door
    to include those whom I have shut out of my concern. . . .
Haunt me with their need.
Burden me with their loneliness
    until I *dare* take responsibility for them,
    until I enlarge the place of my tent.

Jo Carr & Imogene Sorley

~ 37 ~

O Lord, who has taught us that all our doings without charity
    are worth nothing,
Send your Holy Spirit and pour into our hearts
    that most excellent gift of charity,
The very bond of peace and of all virtues,
    without which whoever lives is counted dead before you.
Grant this for your only son Jesus Christ's sake.

Book of Common Prayer

~ *38* ~

Prayer when opening door:
I pray thee, Lord, to open the door of my heart
    to receive thee within my heart.
When washing clothes:
I pray thee, Lord, to wash my heart, making me white as snow.
When sweeping floors:
I pray thee, Lord, to sweep away my heart's uncleanness,
    that my heart may always be pure.
When pouring oil:
I pray thee, Lord, to give me wisdom like the wise virgins who
    always had oil in their vessels.
When posting a letter:
I pray thee, Lord, to add to me faith upon faith,
    that I may always have communication with thee.
When lighting lamps:
I pray thee, Lord, to make my deeds excellent like lamps
    before others, and more, to place thy true light within my heart.
When watering flowers:
I pray thee, Lord, to send down spiritual rain into my heart,
    to germinate the good seed there.
When boiling water for tea:
I pray thee, Lord, to send down spiritual fire
    to burn away the coldness of my heart
    and that I may always be hot-hearted in serving thee.

                    Prayer of Chinese Christian women

～ 39 ～

May God give us light to guide us,
Courage to support us,
And love to unite us,
Now and evermore.

Author unknown

～ 40 ～

For all who watch tonight—by land or sea or air—
O Father, may they know that thou art with them there.
For all who weep tonight, the hearts that cannot rest,
Reveal thy love, that wondrous love which gave for us thy best.
For all who wake tonight, love's tender watch to keep,
Watcher Divine, thyself draw nigh, thou who dost never sleep.

For all who fear tonight, whate'er the dread may be,
We ask for them the perfect peace of hearts that rest in thee.
Our own belov'd tonight, O Father, keep, and where
Our love and succor cannot reach,
  now bless them through ourprayer.
And all who pray tonight, thy wrestling hosts, O Lord,
Make weakness strong, let them prevail according to thy word.

Author unknown

~ 41 ~

For the bread that we have eaten
For the wine that we have tasted
For the life that you have given:
Father, Son and Holy Spirit,
We will praise you.
For the life of Christ within us
Turning all our fears to freedom
Helping us to live for others:
Father, Son and Holy Spirit,
We will praise you. . . .

from Contemporary Prayers for Public Worship

~ 42 ~

O God, the father of lights,
    from whom comes down every good and perfect gift;
Mercifully accept our thanksgivings,
    and look upon our frailty and infirmity,
    and grant us such health of body as you know
    to be needful for us;
That both in body and soul,
    we may evermore serve you with all our strength
    and might.
Through Jesus Christ our Lord.

John Cosin

～ 43 ～

O Lord
My children
My children!
I pray for them so earnestly
So achingly
So imploringly.
Day after day
Year after year
I continue to plead
I continue to intercede.
Are you listening, Lord?
Do you hear me?

Ruth Harms Calkin

～ 44 ～

. . . (Lord,) I do believe; help me overcome my unbelief!

Mark 9:24 (NIV)

~ 45 ~

I have faith in God.
I have faith in Spirit.
I have faith in things invisible.

Charles Fillmore

~ 46 ~

Lord, sometimes thy blessings rain down upon me
    in almost incomprehensible abundance. . . .
But I think I could not bear it, Lord, if every day were like that. . . .
I'm deeply grateful for the ordinary everydays,
    when thy blessings come down upon me gently,
    as summer showers.
There is a calm to such blessings, a time to bask in them.
The *quiet* awareness of your presence brings a *sustaining* strength—
    a strength that enables us to hold steady,
    through both the great moments and the dark nights of the soul.
There's a security and a comfort in the everyday showers of gentle
    blessings.

Jo Carr & Imogene Sorley

~ 47 ~

You take the pen,
and the lines dance.
You take the flute,
and the notes shimmer.
You take the brush,
and the colors sing.
So all things have meaning and beauty
in that space beyond time where you are.
How, then, can I hold anything from you?

Dag Hammarskjold

~ 48 ~

I am unlimited in my power,
and I have increasing health, strength, life, love,
wisdom, boldness, freedom, charity, and meekness
now and forever.
Peace flows like a river through my mind
and I thank thee, O God, that I am one with thee!

Charles & Cora Fillmore

～ 49 ～

I have sinned greatly in what I have done.
Now, O Lord, I beg you, take away the guilt of your servant.
I have done a very foolish thing.

II Samuel 24:10 (NIV)

～ 50 ～

O Lord, increase in me faith and devotion.
Replenish my heart with all goodness,
and by thy great mercy, keep me in the same.
Give me godly zeal in prayer,
true humility in prosperity,
perfect patience in adversity,
and continual joy in the Holy Ghost.

Archbishop Laud

～ 51 ～

. . . Heal her now, O God,
I beseech thee.

Numbers 12:13 (KJV)*

*King James Version

~ 52 ~

Give me this day the eye that is willing to see
    the meaning of the ordinary,
The familiar, the commonplace—
The eye that is willing to see my own faults for what they are—
The eye that is willing to see the likable qualities
    in those I may not like—
The mistake in what I thought was correct—
The strength in what I had labeled as weakness.
Give me the eye that is willing to see that you have not left yourself
    without a witness in every living thing.
Thus to walk with reverence and sensitivity
    through all the days of my life. . . .

Howard Thurman

~ 53 ~

The all-providing substance of Spirit is everywhere present.
I mold it with my thoughts and make it tangible with my faith.

Myrtle Fillmore

~ *54* ~

. . . The Lord is my rock, and my fortress, and my deliverer;
The God of my rock; in him will I trust: he is my shield,
    and the horn of my salvation, my high tower,
    and my refuge, my savior.
Thou savest me from violence.

II Samuel 22:2-4 (KJV)

~ *55* ~

Have mercy on me, O God, have mercy on me,
    for in you my soul takes refuge.
I will take refuge in the shadow of your wings
    until the disaster has passed.
My heart is steadfast, O God,
    my heart is steadfast. . . .

Psalm 57:1, 7 (NIV)

~ 56 ~

Through Jesus Christ I realize my divine sonship,
and I am transformed into his image and likeness.

Charles Fillmore

~ 57 ~

O send your light and your truth,
    that we may live always near to you, our God.
Let us feel your love, that we may be as it were already in heaven,
    that we may do all our work as the angels do theirs.
Let us be ready for every work, be ready to go out or come in,
    to stay or to depart, just as you shall appoint.
Lord, let us have no will of our own, or consider our true happiness
    as depending in the slightest degree on anything
That can befall us outwardly,
    but as consisting altogether in conformity to your will.
Through Jesus Christ our Lord.

Henry Martyn

~ 58 ~

The Lord is slow to anger,
    abounding in love and forgiving sin and rebellion.
Yet he does not leave the guilty unpunished. . . .
In accordance with your great love,
    forgive the sin of these people. . . .

Numbers 14:18, 19 (NIV)

~ 59 ~

Help each one of us, gracious Father, to live in such magnanimity
    and restraint that the Head of the Church
    may never have cause to say to any one of us:
'This is my body, broken by you.'

Author unknown (China)

～ *60* ～

Glory to God in the highest, and on earth peace,
good will toward men.

Luke 2:14 (KJV)

～ *61* ～

Bless Jehovah, O my soul;
And all that is within me, bless his holy name.
Bless Jehovah, O my soul,
And forget not all his benefits:
Who forgiveth all thine iniquities;
Who healeth all thy diseases:
Who redeemeth thy life from destruction;
Who crowneth thee with lovingkindness and tender mercies;
Who satisfieth thy desire with good things,
So that thy youth is renewed like the eagle.

Charles Fillmore

~ *62* ~

I thank you, my creator and Lord,
　　that you have given me these joys in your creation,
　　this ecstasy over the works of your hands.
I have made known the glory of your works to men
　　as far as my finite spirit was able to comprehend your infinity.
If I have said anything wholly unworthy of you,
　　or have aspired after my own glory, graciously forgive me.

Johann Kepler

~ *63* ~

My God, I will rejoice in whatever happens.
All that pleases thee pleases me,
because it is thy will.

Abbe Lasausse

~ *64* ~

Father, let me hold thy hand
and like a child walk with thee down all my days,
Secure in thy love and strength.

Thomas à Kempis

~ *65* ~

O Lord, never allow us to think
that we can stand by ourselves,
and not need you.

John Donne

~ 66 ~

If I have found grace in thy sight,
show me now thy way,
that I may know thee,
that I may find grace in thy sight. . . .

Exodus 33:13 (KJV)

~ 67 ~

O God, who tells the number of the stars,
and calls them all by their names;
Heal, we beg of you, the contrite in heart,
and gather together the outcasts,
and enrich us with the fullness of your wisdom.
Through Christ our Lord.

Sarum Breviary

~ 68 ~

I pray thee, O God, that I may be beautiful within.

Socrates

~ 69 ~

In you, O Lord, I have taken refuge;
    let me never be put to shame;
    deliver me in your righteousness.
Turn your ear to me, come quickly to my rescue;
    be my rock of refuge,
    a strong fortress to save me.
Since you are my rock and my fortress,
    for the sake of your name lead and guide me.
Free me from the trap that is set for me, for you are my refuge.
Into your hands I commit my spirit;
    redeem me, O Lord, the God of truth. . . .

Psalm 31:1-5 (NIV)

~ 70 ~

Lord, all day long
I've acted like a cranky old woman.
I've splattered complaints
In every room of our house. . . .

But now while I get ready for bed
My husband is listening
To his favorite newscaster.
In the background I hear:
"Fire destroys family of six."
"Frantic parents receive ransom note."
"Head-on collision paralyzes woman."
"Pakistan quake kills 7,000."
On and on it goes, dear Lord
And my foolish complaints are shamed.
Forgive my gross selfishness.
Enable me to accept eagerly
My personal responsibilities.
Lord, in some small way tomorrow
May I assuage the world's heartache
Without contributing to it.

Ruth Harms Calkin

~ 71 ~

O Lord, strengthen and support . . .
   all persons unjustly accused or underrated.
Comfort them by the ever-present thought
   that you know the whole truth,
   and will, in your own good time,
   make their righteousness as clear as the light.
Give them grace to pray for such as do them wrong,
   and hear and bless them when they pray.
For the sake of Jesus Christ our Lord and Savior.

Christina Rossetti

~ 72 ~

I cannot be afraid, for God is omnipresent Good.
God is omnipresent protection.
I will fear no evil; for thou art with me.

Myrtle Fillmore

～ *73* ～

Though the fig tree does not bud
    and there are no grapes on the vines,
Though the olive crop fails
    and the fields produce no food,
Though there are no sheep in the pen
    and no cattle in the stalls,
Yet I will rejoice in the Lord,
    I will be joyful in God my Savior. . . .

Habakkuk 3:17–18 (NIV)

～ *74* ～

O God, who art my Father,
I repose in thee as a little child on the breast of his mother.
Thou wilt not abandon me if I serve thee with love.

Abbe Lasausse

~ 75 ~

O heavenly Father, subdue in me whatever
    is contrary to thy holy will.
Grant that I may ever study to know thy will,
    that I may discover how to please thee.
Give me a true understanding and love of thy Word,
    that it may be to me bread which nourisheth to eternal life.
Grant also that I may never run into those temptations
    which in my prayers I desire to avoid;
And never permit my trials, O Lord,
    to be above my strength.

Bishop Thomas Wilson

~ 76 ~

My God, deign to inspire me during prayer
with those reflections I ought to make,
and with the resolutions I ought to form.
Let it be thy holy Spirit who will pray in me.

Abbe Lasausse

∼ 77 ∼

May God himself, the God of peace,
    sanctify you through and through.
May your whole spirit, soul and body be kept blameless
    at the coming of our Lord Jesus Christ

I Thessalonians 5:23 (NIV)

∼ 78 ∼

The Spirit of him that raised up Jesus dwells in me,
    and I am made perfect.

Charles Fillmore

~ 79 ~

O God, our loving Father,
    we pray thee to keep us ever close to thyself,
    that we may find in thy love our strength and our peace.

William Temple

~ 80 ~

Grant us, O Lord, not to mind earthly things,
    but to love things heavenly.
And even now, while we are placed among things
    that are passing away,
    to cleave to those that shall abide.
Through Jesus Christ our Lord.

Leonine Sacramentary

~ *81* ~

Lord, now lettest thou thy servant depart in peace,
  according to thy word.
For mine eyes have seen thy salvation
  which thou hast prepared before the face of all people:
A light to lighten the Gentiles,
  and the glory of thy people Israel.

Luke 2:29-32 (KJV)

~ *82* ~

Keep me safe, O god, for in you I take refuge. . . .

Psalm 16:1 (NIV)

~ 83 ~

And this is my prayer:
    that your love may abound more and more
    in knowledge and depth of insight,
    so that you may be able to discern what is best
    and may be pure and blameless until the day of Christ,
    filled with the fruit of righteousness that comes through
    Jesus Christ—to the glory and praise of God.

Philippians 1:9-11 (NIV)

~ 84 ~

Thy spirit sets me free:
Thou, only, healest me.

Charles Fillmore

~ 85 ~

Teach me, O Father, how to ask you each moment,
    silently, for your help.
If I fail, teach me at once to ask you to forgive me.
If I am disquieted, enable me, by your grace, quickly to turn to you.
May nothing this day come between me and you. . . .

Edward Bouverie Pusey

~ *86* ~

O send out thy light and thy truth: let them lead me;
Let them bring me unto thy holy hill, and to thy tabernacles.
Then will I go unto the altar of God, unto God my exceeding joy.
Yea, upon the harp will I praise thee, O God, my God!

Psalm 43:3–4 (KJV)

~ *87* ~

Into thy hands, O Lord, we commend ourselves this day.
Let thy presence be with us to its close.
Strengthen us to remember that
    in whatsoever good work we do, we are serving thee.
Give us a diligent and watchful spirit
    that we may seek in all things to know thy will,
And knowing it, gladly to perform it.

Author unknown

~ 88 ~

Be, O Lord, our protection, who is our redemption;
Direct our minds by your gracious presence,
    and watch over our paths with guiding love;
That, among the snares which lie hidden in this path
    in which we walk,
        we may so pass onward with hearts fixed on you,
That by the track of faith we may come to be
    where you would have us.

Mozarabic

~ 89 ~

O Lord our God, when the storm is loud, and the night is dark,
    and the soul is sad, and the heart oppressed;
Then, as weary travelers, may we look to thee;
And beholding the light of thy love, may it bear us on,
    until we learn to sing thy song in the night.

George Dawson

~ 90 ~

Lord, the wounds of the world are too deep for us to heal.
We have to bring men and women to you
    and ask you to look after them—
    the sick in body and mind, the withered in spirit,
    the victims of greed and injustice, the prisoners of grief.
And yet, our Father, do not let our prayers excuse us
    from paying the price of compassion.
Make us generous with the resources you have entrusted to us.
Let your work of rescue be done in us and through us all.

from Contemporary Prayers for Public Worship

~ 91 ~

We commend to your lovingkindness, O God,
    all our relations and friends,
    that they may be filled with your grace.
Have mercy on all sick and dying persons,
    all who are suffering or in sorrow.
And grant to all who are living in error, or ignorance, or sin,
    the grace of repentance.
Through Jesus Christ our Lord.

Thomas Thellusson Carter

～ 92 ～

O Lord, you have searched me and you know me.
You know when I sit and when I rise;
You perceive my thoughts from afar.
Before a word is on my tongue
    you know it completely, O Lord.
Search me, O God, and know my heart;
    test me and know my anxious thoughts.
See if there is any offensive way in me,
    and lead me in the way everlasting.

Psalm 139:1-2, 4, 23-24 (NIV)

～ 93 ～

I no longer accuse myself and others of sin and evil.
Forgiving, I am forgiven and healed.
I daily praise the invisible good
    that is bringing the ships of prosperity to my harbor.

Charles & Cora Fillmore

～ *94* ～

Thou has invited me "to ask, to seek, to knock"—
Assuring me that if I ask, it shall be given unto me.
If I seek, I shall find; if I knock, it shall be opened unto me.
Help me to believe that, O God.
Give me the faith to ask knowing that I shall receive.
Give me the faith to seek, believing that I shall surely find.
Give me the faith and the persistence to knock,
    knowing that it shall indeed be opened unto me.
Help me to live the Christian life in daring faith and humble trust,
    that there may be worked out in me, even in me,
    thy righteousness and goodness.
With a sense of adventure, I make this prayer.

Peter Marshall

～ *95* ～

O my divine Savior, fill me with thy spirit.
Grant that I may never speak or act contrary to it.

Abbe Lasausse

~ 96 ~

I love you, O Lord, my strength.
The Lord is my rock, my fortress and my deliverer;
    my God is my rock, in whom I take refuge.
He is my shield and the horn of my salvation, my stronghold.
I call to the Lord, who is worthy of praise,
    and I am saved from my enemies.

Psalm 18:1-3 (NIV)

~ 97 ~

Grant us grace, our Father, to do our work this day
    as workmen who need not be ashamed.
Give us the spirit of diligence and honest enquiry
    in our quest for the truth,
    the spirit of charity in all our dealings with our fellows,
And the spirit of gaiety, courage, and a quiet mind
    in facing all tasks and responsibilities.

Reinhold Niebuhr

～ 98 ～

O Lord, Who hast given unto us thy word of truth:
    quicken within us an increasing love of thy revelation of thyself;
And grant that, delighting daily to exercise ourselves therein,
    and bringing forth fruit as trees of thy planting,
We may be nourished by the waters of thy grace
    and daily be ripening unto everlasting life.

Mozarabic

～ 99 ～

Lord, here I am,
    do with me as seems best in thine own eyes.
Only give me, I humbly beseech thee,
    a penitent and patient spirit to expect thee.
Make my service acceptable to thee while I live,
    and my soul ready for thee when I die.

Archbishop Laud

～ 100 ～

One thing I ask of the Lord, this is what I seek:
    that I may dwell in the house of the Lord
    all the days of my life,
    to gaze upon the beauty of the Lord
    and to seek him in his temple.
I am still confident of this:
I will see the goodness of the Lord in the land of the living.

Psalm 27:4, 13 (NIV)

~ 101 ~

Father,

I've been crying over my child's "spilt milk," which is useless.

He's reached the age where the decisions are his own.

His is the milk, and his is the mess—

and his is the right and the responsibility to clean it up. . . .

He is always my son, Lord—

but his decisions are no longer my responsibility.

It is essential—for his sake—that I let him go.

I believe in him, believe in his ability to come through this crisis. . . .

Why do I deny that belief with motherly blubbering?

Besides, I have promises of my own to keep,

and things to do and miles to go before I sleep.

Watch over my son, Lord.

Jo Carr & Imogene Sorley

~ 102 ~

O Lord, the house of my soul is narrow.

Enlarge it that thou mayest enter in.

It is ruinous. O repair it!

It displeases thy sight—I confess it, I know.

But who shall cleanse it,

or to whom shall I cry but unto thee?

Cleanse me from my secret faults, O Lord,

and spare thy servant from strange sins.

St. Augustine

～ 103 ～

O God, you have wrought this great world with exceeding beauty—
Let there be nothing in our thoughts or actions today
    that will mar that beauty.
Where we can, enable us to replace selfishness
    with imagination and generosity,
       roughness with gentleness, half-truths with your shining truth.
Save us from the temptation to seek gain without service,
    and excitement without considering its cost to others.
Enable us to stand for the difficult right against the easy wrong,
    and the constructive plan that builds up life,
       rather than that which undermines and destroys.
Let your will be done more and more in this world—and in each of us.

Rita F. Snowden

～ 104 ～

How easy for me to live with you, O Lord!
How easy for me to believe in you!
When my mind parts in bewilderment or falters,
When the most intelligent people see no further than this day's end
    and do not know what must be done tomorrow,
You grant me the serene certitude that you exist
    and that you will take care
       that not all the paths of good be closed.

Aleksandr Solzhenitsyn

～ 105 ～

Father,
Grant a special blessing on those who teach our children this year.
Theirs is not an easy task, and it doesn't reap much day-to-day glory.
But the influence they have on my children
    is second only to my own.
Sometimes they can utter a word, and it becomes gospel.
Sometimes they can breathe life into an author
    or an issue or a set of problems, or instill an idea
    that becomes a determining factor for a whole lifestyle.
May they be aware of—and use carefully—
    the power concentrated in them.
And may I remember to express my appreciation, my thanks,
    my gratitude to them.

Jo Carr & Imogene Sorley

～ 106 ～

God grant me the strength
To reach out for my dreams
And see the world
With understanding and love,
And believe in the beauty
Of life and the dignity of mankind.

Andrew Harding Allen

~ *107* ~

Father Almighty!
We bow before thine infinite goodness
    and invoke in prayer thine all-merciful presence of love.

We ask, and as we ask we give thanks
    that thy power and presence are here in love
And that we are tightly held in thine all-embracing arms,
    where our every need is supplied
And where we shall ever rest secure from all the buffets of the world.

Open to us the inner chambers of peace and harmony,
    which divinely belong to us as thy children.

We come as little children into the sacred
    and trustful presence of thy love,
Knowing full well that only love can draw and hold us
    in peace and harmony and prosperity.

Every fear falls away as we enter into thee
    and thy glory of love
And as we bask in the sunshine of love, thy love,
Thy never-failing love!

                    Charles & Cora Fillmore

∼ 108 ∼

Lord, as I hold her in my arms and kiss her tiny fingers
I wonder if anyone in all the world
Has ever been as happy as I am now!
She's like a tiny poem
Short but beautiful—
And several years from now she'll be a story.
Lord, I'm trusting you to write the plot.
Then at last she'll be a book-length novel
Translated into many languages.
I am confident of this, Lord
For you are both Author and Publisher.

Ruth Harms Calkin

∼ 109 ∼

O my Savior, be forever in my thoughts
    by the recollection of thy perfections,
    of thy mysteries, and of thy love.
Be always in my heart by holy affections,
    and by a desire to please thee.
Let me speak thy language, live thy life.

Abbe Lasausse

∾ *110* ∾

Lord God Almighty, shaper and ruler of all creatures,
    we pray for your great mercy,
That you guide us better than we have done, towards you.
And guide us to your will, to the need of our soul,
    better than we can ourselves.
And steadfast our mind towards your will and to our soul's need.
And strengthen us against the temptations of the devil,
    and put far from us all lust, and every unrighteousness,
    and shield us against our foes, seen and unseen.
And teach us to do your will,
    that we may inwardly love you before all things,
    with a pure mind.
For you are our maker and our redeemer,
    our help, our comfort, our trust, our hope.
Praise and glory be to you now, ever and ever, world without end.

Alfred the Great

∾ *111* ∾

Preserve me, Lord, while I am waking,
    and defend me while I am sleeping,
That my soul may continually watch for thee,
    and both body and soul may rest in thy peace forever.

Bishop Cosin

～ 112 ～

Oh, Lord, incomprehensible,
Whom I alternately seek and ignore, forgive my inconstancy.
Sometimes I clamor so childishly at heaven's gates,
    demanding grace. . . .
Oh, God, I don't want this kind of wishy-washy life.
This is not the kind of relationship I want with you at all.
And surely it cannot be the kind of relationship you want with me.
You are there, whether or not I clamor.
You are here.
And my much-ado merely serves to focus my mind on me.
You are with me.
Forgive my inconstancy.
In thee do I trust.

Jo Carr & Imogene Sorley

～ 113 ～

O Lord Jesus Christ, thou Word of God,
Creator and Redeemer,
Possess our mind and conscience,
Our heart and imagination,
By thine indwelling Spirit
That we and all men, being purged of pride,
May find and rest in that love
Which is thy very self.

William Temple

～ 114 ～

God, give us grace to accept with serenity
the things that cannot be changed,
Courage to change the things that should be changed,
and the wisdom to distinguish the one from the other.

Reinhold Niebuhr

～ 115 ～

O Lord our Lord,
how excellent is thy name in all the earth!

Psalm 8:9 (KJV)

∽ 116 ∽

As the deer pants for streams of water,
    so my soul pants for you, O God.
My soul thirsts for God, for the living God.
When can I go and meet with God?
My tears have been my food day and night,
    while men say to me all day long,
"Where is your God?"

Psalm 42:1-3 (NIV)

∽ 117 ∽

Look upon us, O Lord, and let all the darkness of our souls
    vanish before the beams of your brightness.
Fill us with holy love, and open to us the treasures of your wisdom.
All our desire is known unto you,
    therefore perfect what you have begun,
    and what your Spirit has awakened us to ask in prayer.
We seek your face; turn your face unto us and show us your glory,
    then shall our longing be satisfied,
    and our peace shall be perfect.
Through Jesus Christ our Lord.

St. Augustine

~ 118 ~

We bless you, O God, for work that leads us forth in the morning—
and brings us home at night.
We bless you for good relationships,
and interests and skills shared at work and at play.
We bless you for books and papers, TV and radio,
and all that enlarges our knowledge, and widens our horizons.
Enable us to receive these wonderful gifts and use them well—
with discipline and discrimination.

Rita F. Snowden

~ 119 ~

O God our Father, who hast made us in thine own image,
with a mind to understand thy works,
a heart to love thee, and a will to serve thee:
Increase in us that knowledge, love, and obedience,
that we may grow daily in thy likeness.

G. W. Briggs

∽ 120 ∽

Bless our children with healthful bodies,
With good understandings,
With the graces and gifts of your Spirit,
With sweet dispositions and holy habits;
And sanctify them throughout in their bodies, souls, and spirits;
And keep them unblamable to the coming of our Lord Jesus.

Jeremy Taylor

∽ 121 ∽

My mind is stayed on thee,
and I rest in thy peace and power.

Charles Fillmore

∽ 122 ∽

May God bless you with good health and close friends
    every day the whole day through.
May God protect you and look after the loved ones around you.
May God love you and always be near, wherever you go.

Arida Fuller

〜 *123* 〜

Joy!
My favorite word.
Circumstances may determine my happiness,
But, Lord, you determine my joy.
Joy is sweetly honest.
No wonder the minister said:
"You can't hide joy if you have it—
You can't fake it if you don't."
Who can manufacture it, Lord?
Joy is your creation.
Who may have it?
Anyone who asks.
Thank you, Lord
For joy!

Ruth Harms Calkin

〜 *124* 〜

. . . I will sing to the Lord for he is highly exalted. . . .
The Lord is my strength and my song;
he has become my salvation.
He is my God, and I will praise him. . . .

Exodus 15:1–2 (KJV)

～ 125 ～

We pray thee, Lord,
Who art the author and giver of light,
That thou wouldst banish from us this day
    the shadows of evil,
And shed upon us the bright beams
    of thy loving-kindness.

Gelasian Sacramentary

～ 126 ～

Holy One, I would do thy will;
I would give all that I am, all that I am capable of being,
    into thy keeping.
I would think thy thoughts after thee.
I would give my life in making manifest thy will
    in all my words and work.
I would be dependent on thee alone
    for my inspiration and incentive.
I would know and acknowledge no other source.
Thou has sent me into the world;
Thou only canst direct and vitalize my effort.
Help me to realize this momently:
There is none beside thee.

Myrtle Fillmore

~ *127* ~

Good morning Lord, I'm ready
To start a brand new day.
Keep me calm in spite of all
I'm bound to face today.
Seal my lips 'lest I should put
My foot into my mouth.
Give me the strength to do my job,
Though in the North or South.

Good morning, Lord, I'm back again.
I've had a good night's sleep.
Perhaps things might run smoother
If you will help me keep
My temper and my senses
Until the day is through.
Help me forget my troubles
And concentrate on you.

Grace E. Easley

~ *128* ~

Lord, I would sigh only for thee.
Grant that I may see but thee,
That I may feel but thee, taste but thee,
Think but of thee, speak and work but for thee.
Thou art my treasure; let my heart repose in thee.

Abbe Lasausse

～ 129 ～

Show me, O Lord, my life's end and the number of my days;
    let me know how fleeting is my life.
You have made my days a mere handbreadth;
    the span of my years is as nothing before you.
Each man's life is but a breath.
Man is a mere phantom as he goes to and fro;
    he heaps up wealth, not knowing who will get it.
But now, Lord, what do I look for? My hope is in you.
Save me from all my transgressions;
    do not make me the scorn of fools.
Hear my prayer, O Lord, listen to my cry for help;
    be not deaf to my weeping. . . .

Psalm 39:4-8, 12 (NIV)

～ 130 ～

Teach us, good Lord,
To serve thee as thou deservest;
To give and not to count the cost;
To fight and not to heed the wounds;
To toil and not to seek for rest;
To labor and not to ask for any reward
Save that of knowing that we do thy will.

St. Ignatius of Loyola

~ *131* ~

Hear my voice when I call, O Lord;
    be merciful to me and answer me.
My heart says of you, "Seek his face!"
Your face, Lord, I will seek.

Psalm 27:7 (NIV)

~ *132* ~

Eternal God, who hast been the hope and joy of many generations,
and in all ages hast given men the power to seek thee
and in seeking to find thee:
grant me, I pray thee, a clearer vision of thy truth,
a greater faith in thy power,
and a more confident assurance of thy love.

If I cannot find thee, let me search my heart
and know whether it is not rather I that am blind—
than thou who art obscure,
and I who am fleeing from thee
rather than thou from me.
And let me confess these my sins before thee,
and seek thy pardon in Jesus Christ my Lord.

John Baillie

~ *133* ~

Lord, you have been our dwelling place throughout all generations.

Before the mountains were born or you brought forth the earth and
    the world, from everlasting to everlasting you are God.

The length of our days is seventy years—or eighty, if we have the
    strength; yet their span is but trouble and sorrow,
      for they quickly pass, and we fly away.

Teach us to number our days aright,
      that we may gain a heart of wisdom.

Satisfy us in the morning with your unfailing love,
      that we may sing for joy and be glad with all our days.

May your deeds be shown to your servants,
      your splendor to their children.

May the favor of the Lord our God rest upon us;
      establish the work of our hands for us—yes, establish the work
of our hands.

Psalm 90:1-2, 10, 12, 14, 16-17 (NIV)

~ *134* ~

O God, our help in ages past, our hope for years to come,
Our shelter from the stormy blast, and our eternal home!
Under the shadow of thy throne, still may we dwell secure;
Sufficient is thine arm alone, and our defense is sure. . . .
O God, our help in ages past, our hope for years to come,
Be thou our guide while life shall last, and our eternal home!

Isaac Watts

~ *135* ~

O God, I rejoice that all the people I shall meet today are your people.
Let none in need of friendship, or any gift I have to give,
    feel he is a nuisance;
Let no child with his honest questions find me less than honest;
Let no . . . lonely person, with a spate of talk,
    find me unwilling to listen.
Quicken my imagination, and my sympathy,
    that I may begin to see what life is for each of these—
    and what it might become.
Save my tongue from gossip and my hands from idleness.
Create in me a steady belief in things good and true and lovely,
    that all who come my way may get a glimpse
    of your kingdom on earth.

Rita F. Snowden

~ *136* ~

My God, I beg of thee to empty my heart of all vanity,
    of all affection for things perishable,
So that thou mayest become absolute master thereof,
    and do with me as thou wilt.

Abbe Lasausse

~ *137* ~

I arise today with the power of God to guide me,
The might of God to uphold me,
The wisdom of God to teach me,
The eye of God to watch over me,
The ear of God to hear me,
The word of God to give me speech,
The hand of God to protect me,
The way of God to prevent me,
The shield of God to shelter me,
And the host of God to defend me:
Against the snares of devils,
Against the temptations of vices,
Against the lusts of nature,
Against every man who meditates injury to me,
Whether far or near, with few or with many.

St. Patrick

~ *138* ~

Dear God
As the luminous sky
Holds a million scattered stars
Please hold my scattered thoughts
And illumine them *with you.*

Ruth Harms Calkin

～ 139 ～

O God, it is easy to give thanks when things go well,
    and we share the comfort of home
    and the peace and beauty of our situation.
But never let us forget the homeless ones, those who suffer,
    those who are lonely or fearful.
And never let us forget when we hush our hearts in your presence,
    those at this moment distraught
    amid the mad destruction of war.
Let our new knowledge, O God, issue in new ways—
    ways of mutual life and happiness.

Rita F. Snowden

～ 140 ～

The Lord enrich us with his grace,
    and further us with his heavenly blessing.
The Lord defend us in adversity
    and keep us from all evil.
The Lord receive our prayers,
    and graciously absolve us from our offences.

Gregorian Sacramentary

～ 141 ～

. . . Father, forgive them, for they know not what they do.

Luke 23:34 (KJV)

~ 142 ~

Have mercy on me, O God, according to your unfailing love;
according to your great compassion blot out my transgressions.
Wash away all my iniquity and cleanse me from my sin.
Surely you desire truth in the inner parts;
you teach me wisdom in the inmost place.
Create in me a pure heart, O God, and renew a steadfast spirit within me.
Do not cast me from your presence or take your Holy Spirit from me.
Restore to me the joy of your salvation and grant me a willing spirit,
to sustain me.
O Lord, open my lips, and my mouth will declare your praise.
You do not delight in sacrifice, or I would bring it;
you do not take pleasure in burnt offerings.
The sacrifices of God are a broken spirit; a broken and contrite heart.
O God, you will not despise.

Psalm 51:1-2, 6, 10-12, 15-17 (NIV)

~ 143 ~

O God, by whom the meek are guided in judgement,
    and light riseth up in darkness for the godly:
Grant us, in all our doubts and uncertainties,
    the grace to ask what thou wouldest have us to do;
That the Spirit of wisdom may save us from all false choices,
    and that in thy light we may see light
And in thy straight path may not stumble.

William Bright

~ *144* ~

Grant, O Lord, that we may be diligent to read thy word,
Wherein is wisdom, wherein is the royal law,
Wherein are the lively oracles of God;
And that reading it,
We may daily increase in the knowledge of thyself,
And love and serve thee with more perfect heart.

Author unknown

~ *145* ~

O thou who art the strength of souls,
    guide us through the darkness of this world.
Guard us from its perils.
Hold us up and strengthen us
    when we grow weary in our mortal way;
And lead us by thy chosen paths
    to our eternal home in thy heavenly kingdom.

Hebrew Liturgy

~ *146* ~

Atop the ridge of earthly fame,
I look back in wonder at the path
    which I alone could never have found,
A wondrous path through despair to this point from which I, too,
    could transmit to mankind a reflection of your rays.
And as much as I must still reflect
    you will give me.
But as much as I cannot take up
    you will have already assigned to others.

Aleksandr Solzhenitsyn

~ *147* ~

Eternal Father, forgive me that so often I'm in such a hurry:
That my day begins in a scramble without proper time for praise;
That my personal affairs are made to seem
    more important than anybody else's;
That I wade into my work with its human relationships
    without proper care.
Forgive me if I am ever over-confident.
Forgive me if I am ever unreliable.
Forgive me if I am at times over-critical.
If there are decisions I have delayed, let me act today.
If there are letters still unanswered, let me write at once.
If there are habits I mean to give up, let me start now.
Command my temper and my tongue this day.
For Christ's sake.

Rita F. Snowden

～ *148* ～

O Lord, our God, teach us, we beg of you,
    to ask you in the right way for the right blessings.
Steer the vessel of our life towards yourself,
    tranquil haven of all storm-tossed souls.
Show us the course in which we should go.
Renew a willing spirit within us.
Let your Spirit curb our wayward senses,
    and guide and enable us unto that which is our true good,
To keep your laws, and in all our works evermore to rejoice
    in your glorious and gladdening presence.
For yours is the glory and praise from all your saints, forever and ever.

St. Basil

～ *149* ～

O Lord, let me not henceforth desire health or life,
    except to spend them for you, with you, and in you.
You alone know what is good for me;
    do therefore, what seems best.
Give to me, or take from me;
    conform my will to yours;
And grant that, with humble and perfect submission,
    and in holy confidence,
I may receive the orders of your eternal providence,
    and may equally adore all that comes to me from you.
Through Jesus Christ our Lord.

Blaise Pascal

～ 150 ～

O thou Lover of mankind,
Send down into our hearts that peace
Which the world cannot give,
And give us peace in this world.
O King of Peace,
Keep us in love and charity.
Be our God, for we have none other beside thee.
Grant unto our souls the life of righteousness
That the death of sin may not prevail against us,
Or against any of thy people.

W.P. Hook

～ 151 ～

Gracious Father, we ask your guidance:
For all who are in pain;
For all who are perplexed;
For all who count themselves failures.
Give them courage to keep on.
Give them companionship that they do not struggle alone. . . .
Give them some new shining truth, some new interest,
 and your love to sustain them.
And when the hard day is done, and the shadows long drawn out,
 bring them home in peace.
In the name of Jesus, our Lord.

Rita F. Snowden

~ 152 ~

Be pleased, O Lord, to remember my friends,
 all that have prayed for me, and all that have done me good.
Do thou good to them,
 and return all their kindness double into their own bosom,
Rewarding them with blessings, sanctifying them with thy grace,
 and bringing them at last to thy glory.

After Jeremy Taylor

~ 153 ~

O Lord, hear my prayer,
Fulfil my desire to my good,
And to the praise of thy holy name.

Sarum Breviary

~ 154 ~

Inspire and strengthen us, O Lord God,
By thy Holy Spirit,
To seek thy will and uphold thy honor in all things:
In the purity and joy of our homes,
In the trust and fellowship of our common life,
And in daily service of the good.

E. Milner-White

～ 155 ～

Yet I am always with you;
You hold me by my right hand.
You guide me with your counsel,
    and afterward you will take me into glory.
Whom have I in heaven but you?
And earth has nothing I desire besides you.
My flesh and my heart may fail,
    but God is the strength of my heart
    and my portion forever.

Psalm 73:23-26 (NIV)

～ 156 ～

I am a child of God,
and I am joint heir with Jesus to abiding life,
wisdom, love, peace, substance, strength, and power.

Charles Fillmore

~ 157 ~

So may we be mature in our faith, childlike but never childish,
    humble but never cringing, understanding but never conceited.
So help us, O God, to live and not merely to exist,
    that we may have joy in our work.
In your name, who alone can give us moderation
    and balance and zest for living, we pray.

Peter Marshall

~ 158 ~

Grant unto us, O Lord, the gift of modesty.
When we speak, teach us to give our opinion quietly and sincerely.
When we do well in work or play, give us a sense of proportion,
    that we be neither unduly elated nor foolishly self-deprecatory.
Help us in success to realize what we owe to thee
    and to the efforts of others:
In failure, to avoid dejection;
And in all ways to be simple and natural, quiet in manner and lowly
    in thought.
Through Christ.

Joseph L. Bernardin

~ *159* ~

Praise awaits you, O god, in Zion;
>to you our vows will be fulfilled.

O you who hear prayer, to you all men will come.

You answer us with awesome deeds of righteousness,

O God our savior,
>the hope of all the ends of the earth and of the farthest seas,

>who formed the mountains by your power,

>having armed yourself with strength,

>who stilled the roaring of the seas, the roaring of their waves,

>and the turmoil of the nations.

Those living far away fear your wonders;
>where morning dawns and evening fades

>you call forth songs of joy.

You care for the land and water it; you enrich it abundantly.

The streams of God are filled with water to provide the
>people with grain, for so you have ordained it.

Psalm 65:1-2, 5-9 (NIV)

~ *160* ~

You are worthy, our Lord and God,
>to receive glory and honor and power,

>for you created all things,

>and by your will they were created and have their being.

Revelation 4:11 (NIV)

~ 161 ~

Most loving Savior, we would abide in thee.
Make our hearts thy dwelling place.
Fill our minds with the thought,
    and our imaginations with the picture of thy love.
Take away whatever in us of selfishness or weakness
    hinders our hearing or obeying thy call.
Teach us day by day to live closer to thy side,
    which was pierced that we might live.

William Temple

~ 162 ~

Show me thy ways, O Lord; teach me thy paths.
Lead me in thy truth, and teach me:
    for thou art the God of my salvation;
    on thee do I wait all the day.
Remember, O Lord, thy tender mercies
    and thy lovingkindnesses; for they have been ever of old.
Remember not the sins of my youth, nor my transgressions;
    according to thy mercy remember thou me
    for thy goodness' sake, O Lord.

Psalm 25:4-7 (KJV)

~ *163* ~

Almighty God, who in thy wisdom
Has so ordered our earthly life
That we needs must walk by faith and not by sight:
Grant us such faith in thee that,
Amidst all things that pass our understanding,
We may believe in thy fatherly care,
And ever be strengthened by the assurance
That underneath are the everlasting arms.

Author unknown

~ *164* ~

I beseech thee, O Lord, remember now
how I have walked before thee in truth
and with a perfect heart,
and have done that which is perfect in thy sight.
And Hezekiah wept sore.

. . . Thus saith the Lord . . . "I have heard thy prayer,
I have seen thy tears: behold, I will heal thee. . . .

II Kings 20:3, 5 (KJV)

~ *165* ~

Lord of my aching heart:
He was so young
So very young
With all of life before him.
Exuberant, vital
Full of promise, of breathless wonder.
Gifted, intelligent, sensitive
Always inquisitive
Eager to learn, to know, to do. . . .
Admired by his teachers
Extolled by his friends
Loved, so dearly loved.

Lord, no longer dare I beat my fists
Upon the walls of Heaven.
I am too weary, too sorrow-consumed.
I know now that ten thousand whys
Will never bring him back.
In pitch darkness I have shouted my whys.
My reward? A sea of shadowed silence.
What is left?
What more shall I ask?
Just this, dear God:
Think through me your thoughts.
Create within me your peace
Until there is born in my aching heart
"The trust of the unexplained."

Ruth Harms Calkin

~ *166* ~

O Lord Almighty, God of Israel,
    you have revealed this to your servant, saying,
    "I will build a house for you."
So your servant has found courage to offer you this prayer.
O Sovereign Lord, you are God!
Your words are trustworthy,
    and you have promised these good things to your servant.
Now be pleased to bless the house of your servant,
    that it may continue forever in your sight;
    for you, O Sovereign Lord, have spoken,
    and with your blessing the house of your servant
    will be blessed forever.

II Samuel 7:27-29 (NIV)

~ *167* ~

Grant us, O Lord God, the knowledge of your divine words
    and fill us with the understanding of your holy gospel
    and the riches of your divine gifts
    and the indwelling of your Holy Spirit.
And help us with joy to keep your commandments
    and accomplish them
    and fulfil your will and to be accounted worthy
    of the blessings and the mercies
    that are from you now and at all times.

Syrian Jacobites

~ *168* ~

Comfort, O merciful Father, by your Word and Holy Spirit,
All who are afflicted or distressed, and so turn their hearts unto you,
That they may serve you in truth, and bring forth fruit to your glory.
Be, O Lord, their succor and defense.
Through Jesus Christ our Lord.

Philip Melancthon

~ *169* ~

Almighty and everlasting God, the Comfort of the sad,
    the Strength of sufferers;
Let the prayers of those that cry out of any tribulation
    come unto thee;
That all may rejoice to find that thy mercy is present with them
    in their afflictions.

Author unknown

～ 170 ～

O God of love, who through thy Son hast given us
A new commandment that we should love one another,
Even as thou didst love us, the unworthy and the wandering,
And gavest him up for our redemption:
We pray thee, Lord, to give us thy servants,
In all the time of our life on earth,
A mind forgetful of past ill-will,
And a single heart to love our brethren.

From the Coptic

～ 171 ～

My God, grant that thy grace may abound
    where iniquity has abounded.
Grant that thy love may reign in hearts
    where the love of the world has reigned.
I love thee: I will love all things in thee and for thee.

Abbe Lasausse

~ 172 ~

Lord of Life, we can never be thankful enough
    that you have given us each other.
It is wonderful that we need not face this day alone,
    but can plan and proceed to our tasks together.
More than belonging to each other—bound by ties of love and caring—
    we belong to you, and to your great world family.
Let no selfishness of ours shut us off from any today.

Rita F. Snowden

~ 173 ~

May the Lord make your love increase and overflow for each other
and for everyone else, just as ours does for you.

I Thessalonians 3:12 (NIV)

～ 174 ～

Lord Jesus, merciful and patient, grant us grace, I beseech thee,
    ever to teach in a teachable spirit;
Learning along with those we teach,
    and learning from them whenever thou so pleasest.
Word of God, speak to us, speak by us, what thou wilt.
Wisdom of God, instruct us, instruct by us, if and whom thou wilt.
Eternal Truth, reveal thyself to us, in whatever measure thou wilt;
That we and they may all be taught of God.

Christina Rossetti

～ 175 ～

All through this day, O Lord,
May I touch as many lives as thou
Wouldst have me touch for thee.
And those whom I touch,
Do thou with thy Holy Spirit quicken,
Whether by the word I speak,
The letter I write,
The prayer I breathe,
Or the life I live.

Author unknown

~ *176* ~

For this new morning with its light,
Father, we thank thee.
For rest and shelter of the night,
Father, we thank thee.
For health and food, for love and friends,
For everything thy goodness sends,
Father in heaven, we thank thee.

Ralph Waldo Emerson

~ *177* ~

May the grace of the Lord Jesus sanctify us
and keep us from all evil;
May he drive far from us all hurtful things,
and purify both our souls and our bodies.
May he bind us to himself by the bond of love,
and may his peace abound in our hearts.

Gregorian Sacramentary

~ *178* ~

Praise be to the God and Father of our Lord Jesus Christ,
who has blessed us in the heavenly realms
with every spiritual blessing in Christ.

Ephesians 1:3 (NIV)

~ 179 ~

O god, you know our desperate need for your gift of understanding
    and forgiveness in order to live in harmony with our neighbors.
You know how repeatedly and hopelessly we forget your love for us,
    and turn back continually to ourselves
      as though your love were not to be trusted.
We confess that we have nourished grievances and irritations
    which we ought to forgive.
We have sinfully thought our differences too great for reconciliation;
    and our community is wounded
      by our selfishness, prejudice and pride. . . .
Since you are love, and the source of all love,
    give us strength to leave the easy path of self-satisfaction.
Grant us the courage to forgive as we hope to be forgiven.
And in your mercy heal our divisions and make us whole, together,
    in the love which we have from you.
Through Jesus Christ our Lord.

William Booth

~ 180 ~

Lord, keep my parents in your love.
Lord, bless them and keep them.
Lord, please let me have money and strength and keep my parents
    for many more years so that I can take care of them.

Prayer of a young Ghanaian Christian

～ 181 ～

Pour upon us, O Lord,
    the spirit of brotherly kindness and peace;
So that, sprinkled with the dew of your benediction,
    we may be made glad by your glory and grace.
Through Christ our Lord.

Sarum Breviary

～ 182 ～

Almighty God,
Give us wisdom to perceive thee,
Intellect to understand thee,
Diligence to seek thee,
Patience to wait for thee,
Vision to behold thee,
A heart to meditate upon thee,
And life to proclaim thee.

St. Benedict

～ 183 ～

God is our refuge and strength, an ever-present help in trouble.
Therefore we will not fear, though the earth give way
and the mountains fall into the heart of the sea,
though its waters roar and foam
and the mountains quake with their surging.

Psalm 46:1–3 (KJV)

～ 184 ～

O Lord
May I believe in the darkness
When all hope has vanished
When waves beat with fury
And no star lights my sky.
May I believe without
Feeling or knowing or proving
Till one shining moment when
You shatter the darkness
And all I believed for
Is suddenly mine.

Ruth Harms Calkin

~ 185 ~

Use me, my Savior, for whatever purpose
  and in whatever way thou mayest require.
Here is my poor heart, an empty vessel:
  fill it with thy grace.
Here is my sinful and troubled soul:
  quicken it and refresh it with thy love.
Take my heart for thine abode;
  my mouth to spread abroad the glory of thy Name;
  my love and all my powers
  for the advancement of thy believing people;
And never suffer the steadfastness
  and confidence of my faith to abate.

Dwight L. Moody

~ 186 ~

O thou who art peace eternal,
  and givest peace to those who are steadfast in heart:
Let thy peace be upon us thy servants,
  that in the doing of thy will
  we may ourselves find peace,
  and ever be ministers of peace to others.
Through Jesus Christ our Lord.

Frederick B. Macnutt

～ 187 ～

O heavenly Father, I praise and thank you
    for the peace of the night.
I praise and thank you for this new day.
I praise and thank you for all your goodness and faithfulness
    throughout my life.
You have granted me many blessings.
Now let me accept tribulation from your hand.
You will not lay on me more than I can bear.
You make all things work together for good for your children.

Dietrich Bonhoeffer

～ 188 ～

O God our Father,
We thank thee for uniting our lives,
    and for giving us to each other in the fulfilment of love.
Watch over us at all times.
Guide and protect us, and give us patience as we hold
    each other's hand in thine every moment
    of every day and night,
    and draw strength from thee and from each other.

Frederick B. Macnutt

~ *189* ~

I am afflicted, O amiable Jesus,
    because thou art so little loved and so often offended.
Master of hearts! Take possession of our hearts.
Grant that I may always think of thee, desire only to please thee.
That in all things I may seek only thy glory,
    and endeavor always to love thee and cause others to love thee.

Abbe Lasausse

~ *190* ~

We beseech thee, O Lord,
To set our feet in a large place,
Where hearts are made pure by faith in thee,
And faces are turned to the light:
Where all men are one in thee,
And no narrow walls between man and man destroy
The unity thou hast made in the Spirit of thy Son,
Jesus Christ our Lord.

Author unknown

～ 191 ～

O Lord, who art as the shadow of a great rock in a weary land;
Who beholdst thy weak creatures, weary of labor, weary of pleasure,
    weary of hope deferred, weary of self;
In thine abundant compassion and unutterable tenderness,
    bring us unto thy rest.

Christina Rossetti

～ 192 ～

Strengthen our souls,
    animate our cold hearts with your warmth and tenderness,
    that we may no more live as in a dream,
    but walk before you as pilgrims in earnest to reach their home.
And grant us all at last to meet with your holy saints before your
    throne, and there rejoice in your love for ever and ever.

Gerhard Tersteegen

～ 193 ～

. . . Lord, have patience with me, and I will pay thee all.

Matthew 18:26 (KJV)

~ 194 ~

My God, I believe in thee: increase my faith.
I hope in thee: strengthen my hope.
I love thee, and desire to love thee more and more,
And above all things, and all others for thee:
Quicken my love and make me wholly thine.

Author unknown

~ 195 ~

. . . God of our Lord Jesus Christ . . . give you
the spirit of wisdom and revelation,
so that you may know him better . . .
also that the eyes of your heart may be
enlightened in order that you
may know the hope to which he has called you,
the riches of his glorious inheritance in the saints,
and his incomparably great power for us who believe. . . .

Ephesians 1:17-19 (NIV)

∼ 196 ∼

O Thou full of compassion, I commit and commend myself
    unto thee, in whom I am, and live, and know.
Be thou the Goal of my pilgrimage, and my Rest by the way.
Let my soul take refuge from the crowding turmoil of worldly
    thought beneath the shadow of thy wings.
Let my heart, this sea of restless waves, find peace in thee, O God.

St. Augustine

∼ 197 ∼

You are my lamp, O Lord;
the Lord turns my darkness into light. . . .
. . . the word of the Lord is flawless.
He is a shield for all who take refuge in him.

II Samuel 22:29, 31 (NIV)

～ *198* ～

Help us to understand that the pilgrimage of this life is
    but an introduction, a preface, a training school for what is to come.
Then shall we see all of life in its true perspective.
Then shall we not fall in love with the things of time,
    but come to love the things that endure.
Then shall we be saved from the tyranny of possessions
    which we have no leisure to enjoy,
    of property whose care becomes a burden.
Give us, we pray, the courage to simplify our lives.

Peter Marshall

～ *199* ～

Almighty and eternal God, so draw our hearts to thee,
    so guide our minds, so fill our imaginations, so control our wills
    that we may be wholly thine, utterly dedicated unto thee.
And then use us, we pray thee, as thou wilt,
    but always to thy glory and the welfare of thy people.

William Temple

～ 200 ～

O God, our Father, when we talk to you in prayer
    we can be completely honest
Because you know all our inmost thoughts;
Because you understand us better than anyone;
Because we are not afraid you will be so angry you will not forgive us.
We are truly sorry for the silly things, the mean things,
    the wrong things we've done.
With your loving forgiveness, wash them—
Out of our minds, and out of our hearts;
Out of our thoughts about this day;
And give us strength to do much better.
When we put our heads on our pillows and pull up the covers,
    give us your good gift of sleep—
    and keep us safe til morning light.
For your love's sake.

Rita F. Snowden

～ 201 ～

God be in my head, and in my understanding.
God be in mine eyes, and in my looking.
God be in my mouth, and in my speaking.
God be in my heart, and in my thinking.
God be at mine end, and at my departing.

Sarum Primer

～ 202 ～

. . . O Lord, have mercy on me;
heal me, for I have sinned against you.

Psalm 41:4 (NIV)

~ *203* ~

Out of the depths I cry to you, O Lord;
O Lord, hear my voice.
Let your ears be attentive
      to my cry for mercy.
If you, O Lord, kept a record of sins,
O Lord, who could stand?
But with you there is forgiveness. . . .

Psalm 130:1-4 (NIV)

~ *204* ~

Forgive them all, O Lord. . . :
Our sins of omission and our sins of commission;
The sins of our youth and the sins of our riper years;
The sins of our souls and the sins of our bodies;
Our secret and our more open sins;
Deliberate and presumptuous sins;
The sins we have done to please ourselves
      and the sins we have done to please others;
The sins we know and remember, and the sins we have forgotten;
The sins we have striven to hide from others
      and the sins by which we have made others offend.
Forgive them, O Lord,
      forgive them all for his sake who died for our sins
      and rose for our justification, and now stands at your right hand
      to make intercession for us, Jesus Christ our Lord.

John Wesley

～ 205 ～

Help me, Lord, to remember
That religion is not to be confined
To the church or closet,
Nor exercised only in prayer or meditation,
But that everywhere I am in your presence.
So may my every word and action have a moral content.

Susanna Wesley

～ 206 ～

Blessed Lord, by whose providence all Holy Scriptures
    were written and preserved for our instruction,
Give us grace to study them this and every day,
    with patience and love.
Strengthen our souls with the fulness of their divine teaching.
Keep from us all pride and irreverence.
Guide us in the deep things of your heavenly wisdom,
    and of your great mercy lead us by your word unto everlasting life.
Through Jesus Christ our Lord and Savior.

Bishop Brooke Foss Westcott

~ 207 ~

I AM THAT I AM

Through Jesus Christ I am the master
    of every realm of consciousness in my being.
Through Jesus Christ I enter into a full and complete understanding
    of how to handle all states of consciousness to the glory of God.
I am illumined with the light of Spirit,
    and I bring "every thought into captivity
    to the obedience of Christ."
I commit all my works unto Jehovah,
    and my purposes are established.
Every plane of consciousness in me is transformed
    by the renewing of my mind.

Charles & Cora Fillmore

~ 208 ~

Blessed be God.
My friends are alarmed about the solitariness of my future life,
    and my tendency to melancholy.
But, O my dearest Lord!
You are with me, your rod and your staff they comfort me.
I go on your errand—and I know that you are and will be with me.
How easily can you support and refresh my heart!

Henry Martyn

~ 209 ~

O come, let us sing unto the Lord:
    let us make a joyful noise to the rock of our salvation.
Let us come before his presence with thanksgiving,
    and make a joyful noise unto him with psalms.
For the Lord is a great God, and a great King above all gods.
In his hand are the deep places of the earth:
    the strength of the hills is his also.
The sea is his, and he made it: and his hands formed the dry land.
O come, let us worship and bow down:
    let us kneel before the Lord our maker.
For he is our God; and we are the people of his pasture,
    and the sheep of his hand. . . .

Psalm 95:1-7 (KJV)

~ 210 ~

O Lord of Life,
    we can never be glad enough that we have our home,
    and each other.
Bless all who fall in love today—all who build new homes—
    all who become parents for the first time.
Guide into new ways all who are estranged,
    though they live this day under the same roof.
Bless all the lonely, the broken, the bereaved—
    and all who care for them today.
In Christ's name.

Rita F. Snowden

～ 211 ～

My God, my Love!
Thou art all mine, and I am all thine.
Enlarge me in love;
That with the inner mouth of my heart
I may taste how sweet it is to love.
Let me love thee more than myself,
And myself only for thee,
And in thee all that love thee truly:
As the law of love commandeth shining forth from thee.

Thomas à Kempis

～ 212 ～

Ah, Lord, is this, then, the Christian message?
That I can celebrate life with any other living soul—just because he is,
    as I am, a living soul, and a child of thine?
Ah, so!
I can celebrate life, for it is good. . . .
Lord, I affirm the goodness of life.
And I affirm the goodness of mankind.
For all that is past, I give thanks—
    for it has brought me to this moment.
For all that lies ahead, I say Yes!—
    for thy word is that life is something to rejoice about
    and that the rejoicing can be shared—must be shared.

Jo Carr & Imogene Sorley

~ 213 ~

Praise be to the God and Father of our Lord Jesus Christ,
    the father of compassion and the God of all comfort,
    who comforts us in all our troubles,
    so that we can comfort those in any trouble
    with the comfort we ourselves have received from God.

II Corinthians 1:3-4 (NIV)

~ 214 ~

Almighty God, we earnestly ask you to look upon this household.
Grant that every member of it may be taught and guided of you.
Bless the relations and friends of each of us.
You know their several necessities. . . .

Archibald Campbell Tait

~ 215 ~

God,
I watch my fledgling children perched on the edge of our nest,
    ready and eager and anxious for flight into adulthood—
And I tremble, even as I thrill at the wonder of it all.
Lord, have they learned, somewhere, somehow,
    those things that will hold them steady
    amidst the difficulties and the delights that will be a part of their lives?
Have we protected them too much—or not enough?
Ah, Lord, what is their vision, as they hover on the nest's edge?
Do they sense thy divine scheme of things—
    and the part they can play in it?
I pray this day for them, that they may slip the bonds of child-life,
    and know the joy of flight!

Jo Carr & Imogene Sorley

～ *216* ～

God, give me wisdom, let me understand
That I may teach the needful thing;
Help me to see the hidden, stranger child,
That I life's rightful messages may bring.

God give me patience for the endless task,
The daily repetitions, the slow years
Of molding, line by line, the human mind,
Until at length 'tis free from sordid fears.

God, let me care for those whom I must teach;
Like the great Teacher let me ever love
With tender, brooding, understanding heart,
Eyes wise, farseeing as the stars above.

God, give me faith to see beyond today,
To sow the seed and cultivate the soil;
Then wait serenely, trusting in thy power,
To bless and multiply my humble toil.

An Anonymous Teacher

～ *217* ～

I acknowledge thy presence and power, O blessed Spirit.
In thy divine wisdom now erase my mortal limitations,
And from thy pure substance of love
    bring into manifestation my world,
According to thy perfect law.

Charles & Cora Fillmore

~ 218 ~

God and Father of all, who from the beginning came to bring light
    and truth and love to man, by the Word,
Grant to us who deal with words and images,
    such a reverence for thee,
    that through careful and honest work,
    we may keep the coinage of our language sound.
Give us humility to realize that we are called,
    not to be perfect but to be clear,
    not to be infallible but to be fair.
Direct those who in this our generation speak where many listen,
    who write what many read, and who show what many see,
That they may do their part in making the heart of our people wise,
    its mind sound, and its will righteous.

David B. Collins

~ 219 ~

O God, who resistest the proud,
And givest grace unto the humble:
Grant us the virtue of true humility,
Of which thine only-begotten Son himself
Gave us the perfect example,
That we may never offend thee by our pride,
And be rejected for our self-assertion.

Leonine Sacramentary

～ 220 ～

Lord God of Earth and Sky,
>   whose hand hath harnessed the wind and the rain,
>   whose ear hath marked the pounding of the surf
>   and the small night stir of crickets in the grass;
Bless them this day!
Make thy light to shine upon their faces
>   as they cross the threshold of this wedded life.
Let their souls be the wide windows to the sun
>   and their minds open to the light of mutual understanding.
Let contentment be as a roof over their heads
>   and humility as a carpet for their feet.
Give them love's tenderness for their days of sorrow
>   and love's pride for their days of joy.
Let the voices of children ring sweetly on their ears
>   and the faces of children glow round their hearth-fire.
Let not the evil bird of envy darken their ways
>   or the poisonous fangs of greed sting their hands.
Give them high hearts.
Let beauty dwell with them—in the sheen of copper pans
>   and the cool folding of linen,
In the shining surface of china and tinkle of glass.
Give them, O Lord, these blessings of the simple life.
Make theirs in truth a good marriage—forever and ever.

Author unknown

~ 221 ~

Almighty and Everlasting God, Creator of Heaven,
    Earth and the Universe:
Help me to be, to think, to act what is right, because it is right;
Make me truthful, honest and honorable in all things;
Make me intellectually honest for the sake of right and honor,
    and without thought of reward to me.
Give me the ability to be charitable,
    forgiving and patient with my fellowmen.
Help me to understand their motives and their shortcomings—
    even as thou understandest mine!

Harry S. Truman

~ 222 ~

Into thy hands, O Lord,
    we commend ourselves and all who are dear to us this day.
Be with us in our going out and in our coming in.
Strengthen us for the work which thou has given us to do.
And grant that, filled with thy Holy Spirit,
    we may walk worthy of our high calling,
And cheerfully accomplish those things
    that thou wouldst have done.

Bishop F. T. Woods

∼ 223 ∼

Great and marvelous are your deeds, Lord God Almighty.
Just and true are your ways, King of the ages.
Who will not fear you, O Lord, and bring glory to your name?
For you alone are holy.
All nations will come and worship before you,
 for your righteous acts have been revealed.

Revelation 15:3b–4 (NIV)

∼ 224 ∼

. . . In the beginning, O Lord,
 you laid the foundations of the earth,
 and the heavens are the work of your hands.
They will perish, but you remain;
 they will all wear out like a garment.
You will roll them up like a robe;
 like a garment they will be changed.
But you remain the same,
 and your years will never end.

Hebrews 1:10–12 (NIV)

∼ 225 ∼

The sun has disappeared.
I have switched off the light, and my wife and children are asleep.
The animals in the forest are full of fear,
    and so are the people on their mats.
They prefer the day with your sun to the night.
But I still know that your moon is there,
    and your eyes and also your hands.
Thus I am not afraid.
This day again you led us wonderfully.
Everybody went to his mat satisfied and full.
Renew us during our sleep, that in the morning
    we may come afresh to our daily jobs.
Be with our brothers far away in Asia who may be getting up now.
Amen.

Prayer of a young Ghanaian Christian

∼ 226 ∼

O Lord, who is as the shadow of a great rock in a weary land;
Who beholds your weak creatures, weary of labor, weary of pleasure,
    weary of hope deferred, weary of self:
In your abundant compassion and unutterable tenderness,
    bring us, we pray you, unto your rest.

Christina Rossetti

～ 227 ～

O you who was, and are, and are to come,
I thank you that this Christian way on which I walk
    is no untried or uncharted road, but a road beaten hard
    by the footsteps of saints, apostles, prophets, and martyrs.
I thank you for the finger-posts and danger-signals
    with which it is marked at every turning and which
    may be known to me through the study of the Bible. . . .
Beyond all, I give you devout and humble thanks
    for the great gift of Jesus Christ, the pioneer of our faith . . .
    and that I am not called upon to face any temptation
    or trial which he did not first endure. . . .

John Baillie

～ 228 ～

O Lord, who, in infinite wisdom and love,
    orders all things for your children,
Order everything this day for me in your tender pity.
You know my weakness, who made me.
You know how my soul shrinks from all pain of soul.
Lord, I know you will lay no greater burden on me
    than you can help me to bear.
Teach me to receive all things this day from you.
Enable me to commend myself in all things to you.
Grant me in all things to please you.
Bring me through all things nearer unto you.
Bring me, day by day, nearer to yourself, to life everlasting.

Edward Bouverie Pusey

~ 229 ~

O God, let me know thee and love thee
    so that I may rejoice in thee.
And if I cannot know thee, love thee,
    and rejoice in thee fully in this life,
Let me go forward from day to day,
    until that knowledge, joy, and love at last may be full.
Let the knowledge of thee grow in me here,
    and there be made full.
Let the love of thee increase in me here,
    and there be made full:
So that my joy may here be great in hope,
    and there full in fruition.

St. Anselm

~ 230 ~

The wisdom of the Christ Mind here active
    is through my recognition of Christ
    identified and unified with God.
Wisdom, judgment, discrimination, purity, and power
    are here now expressing themselves in the beauty of holiness.
The justice, righteousness, and peace of the Christ Mind
    now harmonize, wisely direct, and surely establish
    the kingdom of God in his temple, my body.
There are no more warring, contentious thoughts in me,
    for the peace of God is here established,
    and the lion and the lamb (courage and innocence)
    sit on the throne of dominion with wisdom and love.

Charles Fillmore

~ 231 ~

O heavenly Father, open wide the sluice gate into my heart
that I may receive thy living water and be fruitful.

Anonymous Punjabi Christian

~ 232 ~

. . . Lord, you know I love you.

John 21:16 (NIV)

~ 233 ~

Give me the lowest place, not that I dare
Ask for that lowest place, but thou hast died
That I might live and share
Thy glory by thy side.

Give me the lowest place; or if for me
That lowest place too high, make one more low
Where I may sit and see
My God and love thee so.

Christina Rossetti

～ 234 ～

Watch, dear Lord, with those who wake, or watch, or weep tonight,
    and give your angels charge over those who sleep.
Tend your sick ones, O Lord Christ.
Rest your weary ones.
Bless your dying ones.
Soothe your suffering ones.
Pity your afflicted ones.
Shield your joyous ones.
And all, for your love's sake.
Amen.

St. Augustine

～ 235 ～

The Lord bless thee and keep thee:
The Lord make his face shine upon thee, and be gracious unto thee;
The Lord lift up his countenance upon thee, and give thee peace.

Numbers 6:24–26 (KJV)

～ 236 ～

Praise be to the name of God forever and ever;
    wisdom and power are his.
He changes times and seasons;
    he sets up kings and deposes them.
He gives wisdom to the wise and knowledge to the discerning.
He reveals deep and hidden things;
    he knows what lies in darkness,
    and light dwells with him.
I thank and praise you, O God of my fathers. . . .

Daniel 2:20-23 (NIV)

～ 237 ～

We give thee thanks, holy Lord,
Father Almighty, eternal God,
Who has been pleased to bring us
Through the night to the hours of morning.
We pray thee graciously to grant
That we may pass this day without sin,
So that at eventide,
We may again give thanks to thee.

Gelasian Sacramentary

⌒ 238 ⌒

My Lord, I love you.
My God, I am sorry.
My God, I believe in you.
My God, I trust you.
Help us to love one another as you love us.

Mother Teresa of Calcutta

⌒ 239 ⌒

Lord, how is it that *my* child can irritate me
    to the point of distraction,
        doing the very same thing that I would find tolerable—
        even understandable—in my neighbor's child?
Is the act more aggravating with my child than with another?
Or just that I am more uptight about it?

Father, God, grant me the objectivity that I must have
    if I am to be fair with my child.
Help me see him from a little distance.
And help me see him as a person in his own right,
    not as an extension of myself.
I can love and enjoy my child from right here, Lord—
    but help me achieve the distance I need for his discipline.

Jo Carr & Imogene Sorley

～ *240* ～

O Lord, enable me to learn today some things I never knew before,
 to love somebody I never loved before.
Let the spirit which was in Jesus, move within me.
Bless all those who touch my life this day—bless the friendly smile,
 the good plan shared, the pooling of skills. . . .
Where opportunities for joy are close at hand,
 save me from lifting my eyes continually to distant places.
Let the large purposes of your kingdom claim my best gifts,
 the joy of your kingdom, my glad response.
So may this day be enriched for me in giving—
 and for others about me in sharing.
Hasten the day when the ways of war and suffering and confusion
 will give place to justice and peace in the earth.

Rita F. Snowden

～ *241* ～

Lord, I will love my neighbor for thee,
 because he comes from thee, he belongs to thee.
I will always see thee in him, pray for him,
 do for him all the good I can for love of thee.

Abbe Lasausse

~ 242 ~

O Lord God—
In the midst of consuming sorrow
When despair and loneliness hedge me in
You understand my frailties—my hesitancies, my fears.
As I scamper from doubt to doubt
You forgive so quickly my outbursts.
Never do you drive me away
When I rail against you in peevish rebellion.
When I scream "Don't you even care?"
You quiet my fragmented heart,
You work in me silently
Always planning in love.
You refine me in the white-flamed furnace of affliction.
In the silent darkness you whisper:
"Trust me—all will be well."

Ruth Harms Calkin

~ 243 ~

Lord, thou art my refuge, my strength.
I will confide in thee.
I will always depend on thee alone.

Abbe Lasausse

~ *244* ~

My God, my God, why have you forsaken me?
Why are you so far from saving me,
    so far from the words of my groaning?
O my God, I cry out by day, but you do not answer,
    by night, and am not silent.
Do not be far from me, for trouble is near
    and there is no one to help.
But you, O Lord, be not far off:
O my Strength, come quickly to help me.

Psalm 22:1-2, 11, 19 (NIV)

~ *245* ~

. . . O Lord, God of heaven, the great and awesome God,
    who keeps his covenant of love
    with those who love him and obey his commands,
    let your ear be attentive . . . to hear the prayer
your servant is praying before you day and night. . . .

Nehemiah 1:5-6 (NIV)

~ 246 ~

Grant unto us, almighty God,
  the peace of God that passeth understanding,
That we, amid the storms and troubles of this our life,
  may rest in thee, knowing that all things are in thee;
Not beneath thine eye only, but under thy care,
  governed by thy will, guarded by thy love,
So that with a quiet heart we may see the storms of life,
  the cloud and the thick darkness,
Ever rejoicing to know that the darkness and the light
  are both alike to thee.
Guide, guard, and govern us even to the end,
  that none of us may fail to lay hold upon the immortal life.

George Dawson

~ 247 ~

Almighty and everlasting God, be present with us in all our duties,
  and grant the protection of your presence to all that dwell in this house;
That you may be known to be the defender of this household
  and the inhabitants of this dwelling.
Through Jesus Christ our Lord.

Gelasian Sacramentary

~ 248 ~

I am now free from fear, anxiety, worry, dread, and suspense.
I have faith in thy Holy Spirit,
And I trust thee to protect me, to provide for me,
And to bring all my affairs into divine order.

Charles & Cora Fillmore

~ *249* ~

Have mercy, O God, on any for whom this is a bitter dawn—
Any who have parted from a loved one at death;
Any who have been shocked by accident;
Any who find their marriage breaking up.
We are all your children, amid the immensities of life—
We can't manage on our own;
We need your supporting love and care;
We need the kindly support of others about us.
Let no discouragement hinder us from trying again —
Save us from pride that will not own failure;
Save us from hate that has no healing in it;
Save us from speaking words that we will be sorry for later.
Take us into your keeping and teach us anew how to live.

Rita F. Snowden

~ *250* ~

Thou who sendest forth the light, createst the morning,
Makest the sun to rise on the good and on the evil:
Enlighten the blindness of our minds
      with the knowledge of the truth.
Lift thou up the light of thy countenance upon us
      that in thy light we may see light,
And, at the last, in the light of grace,
      the light of glory.

Lancelot Andrewes

~ *251* ~

You've given many gifts, oh Lord,
That brighten, help and cheer,
Like butterflies and sunset skies.
But of gifts there's none more dear
Than pets, dear dogs and cats and all
Who share our smiles and cares
And wag a friendly tail or purr,
Or look with ever caring eyes
Into our own, as though they were
Studying each thought we have.

And when their short, good lives
Are done and they have gone away,
They leave a sorrow. Yes, but too,
A joy that still does stay
On through the years ahead,
And brings a tear but most a smile,
For what they shared with you and me
Helped make our lives worthwhile.

Minnie Boyd Popish

~ 252 ~

The earth is the Lord's, and everything in it,
the world, and all who live in it;
for he founded it upon the seas
and established it upon the waters.

Psalms 24:1-2 (NIV)

~ 253 ~

Almighty and most merciful God,
Who hast given us a new commandment
that we should love one another,
Give us also grace that we may fulfil it.
Make us gentle, courteous, and forbearing.
Direct our lives so that we may look
to the good of others in word and deed.
And hallow all our friendships
by the blessing of thy Spirit.

Bishop Brook Foss Westcott

~ 254 ~

Grant us brotherhood, not only
For this day, but for all our years—
A brotherhood not of words
But of acts and needs.

Stephen Vincent Benet

~ 255 ~

Lord
Please get me off
This emotional elevator
Which carries me so swiftly
From the basement of despair
To the tenth floor of exhilaration
And down to the basement again.
I'm hoarse from shouting.
My fists are blue from pounding.
I'm suffocating in this
Dark windowless box.

Ruth Harms Calkin

~ 256 ~

The water that I live in is full of piranha
and it doesn't do to have a bleeding heart in this locality.
Please God get me out of this water
or give me a shell or teeth . . .
Just don't leave me here with nothing but the conviction
that piranha are all God's children too.

Evangeline Paterson

~ *257* ~

Today, I'm in a hurry, Lord.
There's much I need to do.
Slow me down a while, that I
Might share some time with you.

There are many who are lost, Dear Lord,
Who cannot find their way.
You know each sparrow, man, and child.
Embrace each one, I pray.

Many hurt and hunger, Lord,
I pray thy Will be done.
Slow me down to give you praise,
For blessings, everyone.

As for me, Dear Lord, I cannot ask
For more than you have given.
Slow me down, that I may lift,
My grateful prayers to Heaven.

If any day I fail to pray,
Lord, slow me down a while.
Let me reflect upon your grace,
Before another mile.

Nancy Tant

~ *258* ~

O God, our everlasting hope! . . .
Every work of our hand may we do unto you.
In every trouble, trace some light of yours;
     and let no blessing fall on dry and thankless hearts. . . .
Fill us with patient tenderness for others,
     seeing that we also are in the same case before you.
And make us ready to help, and quick to forgive. . . .

James Martineau

~ *259* ~

Give perfection to beginners, O Father.
Give intelligence to the little ones.
Give aid to those who are running their course.
Give sorrow to the negligent.
Give fervor of spirit to the lukewarm.
Give to the perfect a good consummation.
For the sake of Christ Jesus our Lord.

St. Irenaeus

~ 260 ~

O God, you are my God, earnestly I seek you,
    my soul thirsts for you,
    my body longs for you, in a dry and weary land
    where there is no water.
I have seen you in the sanctuary
    and beheld your power and your glory.
Because your love is better than life, my lips will glorify you.
I will praise you as long as I live,
    and in your name I will lift up my hands.
My soul will be satisfied as with the richest of foods;
    with singing lips my mouth will praise you.

Psalm 63:1–5 (NIV)

~ 261 ~

Lord, you are my lover,
My longing,
My flowing stream,
My sun,
And I am your reflection.

St. Mechthild of Mageburg

∼ 262 ∼

If my hands were not as useful as you would have them be,
Or my feet stood idly waiting or my eyes refused to see,
If my ears were deafened, Lord, to another person's need,
Or I selfishly omitted a kind or thoughtful deed,
I humbly ask forgiveness if I failed in any way
To glorify your goodness as I traveled on my way,
The sun now sets upon a day I know I can't relive.
As for my human failings, I pray, Dear Lord, forgive.
And while I sleep, renew my heart and stir the passion there,
So tomorrow I may glorify the covenant we share. Amen.

Nancy Tant

∼ 263 ∼

We must praise your goodness,
    that you have left nothing undone to draw us to yourself.
But one thing we ask of you, our God,
    not to cease your work in our improvement.
Let us tend towards you, no matter by what means,
    and be fruitful in good works.
For the sake of Jesus Christ our Lord.

Ludwig von Beethoven

~ *264* ~

. . . Blessed be thou, Lord God of Israel
    our father, for ever and ever.
Thine, O Lord, is the greatness, and the power,
    and the glory, and the victory, and the majesty;
For all that is in the heaven and in the earth is thine;
    Thine is the kingdom, O Lord,
And thou art exalted as head above all.

Both riches and honor come of thee,
    and thou reignest over all;
And in thine hand is power and might;
    and in thine hand it is to make great,
And to give strength unto all.
Now therefore, our God, we thank thee,
    and praise thy glorious name.

I Chronicles 29:10–13 (KJV)

~ *265* ~

I have faith in the glorious infusion
of the more abundant life of Christ vitalizing me.
I am lifted up and healed.

Charles Fillmore

~ 266 ~

My God, let me have for thee the heart
 of a child who tenderly loves his father.
Give me for my neighbor the heart of the best of mothers.
For myself, give me the heart of a judge who is most just.

Abbe Lasausse

~ 267 ~

Almighty God, unto whom all hearts be open, all desires known,
 and from whom no secrets are hid;
Cleanse the thoughts of our hearts by the inspiration
 of your Holy Spirit,
 that we may perfectly love you,
 and worthily magnify your holy name.
Through Christ our Lord. Amen.

Leofric, Bishop of Exeter

~ 268 ~

Lord, my God: call me, that I may come to thee.
Fix me, that I may not leave thee.

St. Augustine

~ 269 ~

When I think of your lavish goodness
The longings you've satisfied
The forgiveness you've granted
The promises you've kept;
When I think of Your irresistible love
Your ceaseless care
Your unfailing protection . . .
O Lord God
I want to raise flags and fly banners and sound bugles.
I want to run with lighted torches
And praise you from the mountaintop.
I want to write symphonies and shout for joy.
I want to throw a festive party for ten thousand guests.
I want to celebrate with streamers and bright lights
And an elaborate banquet.

Ruth Harms Calkin

~ 270 ~

God, in his love, fills me with new life.
In his name I am cleansed, strengthened, and healed.

Charles Fillmore

~ 271 ~

O Lord, with whom are strength and wisdom,
    put forth your strength,
I implore you, for your own sake and for our sakes.
And stand up to help us, for we are deceivable and weak persons,
    frail and brief, unstable and afraid,
Unless you put the might of your Holy Spirit within us.

Christina Rossetti

~ 272 ~

Dear Jesus, as a hen covers her chicks with her wings
    to keep them safe,
        do thou this dark night protect us under your golden wings.

Author unknown (India)

~ 273 ~

Restore to me the joy of your salvation
    and grant me a willing spirit to sustain me.

Psalm 51:12 (NIV)

~ 274 ~

Lord, I believe in thee; help thou mine unbelief.
I love thee, yet not with a perfect heart as I would.
I long for thee, yet not with my full strength.
I trust in thee, yet not with my whole mind.
Accept my faith, my love, my longing to know and serve thee,
     my trust in thy power to keep me.
What is cold do thou kindle.
What is lacking do thou make up.
I wait thy blessing.

Malcolm Spencer

~ 275 ~

O heavenly Father,
     the author and fountain of all truth,
Send, we beseech thee,
     Thy Holy Spirit into our hearts,
And lighten our understandings
     with the beams of thy heavenly grace.

Bishop Ridley

~ *276* ~

The clear unclouded mind of Jesus Christ
dominates all my thinking,
And I discern the omnipresent laws of Spirit.

Charles Fillmore

~ *277* ~

Let me live in a house on an ocean shore
Where the surf and sand do meet.
Let me sit, my dear Lord, at the water's edge
Where the waves gently wash my feet.

Let me feel the sun's warmth as it shines on my face;
Watch the sea gulls flying on high.
Let me see the sun set far out in the west
Where the water seems to meet the sky.

But if, my dear Lord, plans that you have for me
Are not plans that I'm dreaming of,
Then thy will be done. I'll be happy to know
I'm forever more bathed in your love.

Albert N. Theel

~ *278* ~

My God, I will all that thou willest.
I rejoice to do what is agreeable to thee.
Let me have but one will with thine.

Abbe Lasausse

～ *279* ～

O God, the renewer and lover of innocency;
Turn the hearts of all your servants to yourself,
  that they may be found ever rooted in faith
  and fruitful in works.
Through Jesus Christ our Lord.

Sarum Breviary

～ *280* ～

O Lord God, holy lover of my soul, when you come into my soul,
 all that is within me shall rejoice.
You are my glory and the exultation of my heart;
You are my hope and refuge in the day of my trouble.
Set me free from all evil passions,
 and heal my heart of all inordinate affections;
That, being inwardly cured and thoroughly cleansed,
 I may be fit to love, courageous to suffer, steady to persevere.
Nothing is sweeter than love, nothing more courageous,
 nothing fuller nor better in heaven and earth;
Because love is born of God, and cannot rest but in God,
 above all things.
Let me love you more than myself, nor love myself but for your sake.

Thomas à Kempis

～ 281 ～

O God, our Refuge in pain, our Strength in weakness,
    our Help in trouble;
We come to thee in our hour of need,
    beseeching thee to have mercy
    upon this thine afflicted servant.
O loving Father, relieve his pain.
Yet if he needs must suffer, strengthen him,
    that he may bear his sufferings with patience
And as his day is, so may his strength be.
Let not his heart be troubled,
    but shed down upon him the peace
    which passeth understanding.
Though now for a season, if need be, he is in heaviness
    through his manifold trials, yet comfort him,
    O Lord, in all his sorrows,
And let his mourning be turned into joy,
    and his sickness into health.

E.B. Pusey

～ 282 ～

Hear my cry, O God; listen to my prayer.
From the ends of the earth I call to you,
I call as my heart grows faint;
    lead me to the rock that is higher than I.
For you have been my refuge, a strong tower against the foe.
I long to dwell in your tent forever
    and take refuge in the shelter of your wings.

Psalm 61:1-4 (NIV)

~ 283 ~

I do not believe in evil. I believe in Good.
I do not believe in sin. I believe in Truth.
I do not believe in want. I believe in Abundance.
I do not believe in death. I believe in Life.
I do not believe in ignorance. I believe in Intelligence.
There are no discords in my being. Being is peace.
My faith, understanding, and love are one.

Myrtle Fillmore

~ 284 ~

Praise God, from whom all blessings flow.
Praise him all creatures here below.
Praise him above, angelic host.
Praise Father, Son, and Holy Ghost.

Thomas Ken

~ 285 ~

My Lord and my God!

John 20:28 (NIV)

~ *286* ~

Save me from leading an imaginary life in the ideas of others,
   and so to be eager and forward in showing myself to the world.
Forbid that I should retain, improve and adorn this fictitious being,
   while stupidly neglecting the truth.
Help me not to contend with men's interests, prejudices,
   and passions, that rarely admit of a calm dispute,
   when it can be innocently avoided.
May I be so far a lover of myself as to prefer the peace
   and tranquillity of my own mind before that of others,
And if, after doing all that I can to make others happy,
   they yet remain obstinately bent to follow
   those ways that lead to misery,
I leave them to your mercy.

Susanna Wesley

~ *287* ~

From the cowardice that dare not face new truth
From the laziness that is contented with half truth
From the arrogance that thinks it knows all truth
Good Lord, deliver me.

Author unknown (Kenya)

~ 288 ~

You know, O Lord, the concerns, the feelings,
    the anxieties of mankind.
Bless them.
Bless those who are victims of illnesses they strive to conquer.
Bless those who have fallen from grace
    and whose burdens are beyond their strength to bear.
Open my eyes to possibilities that are hidden.
Enlarge my heart that I may hold in my prayers the hopes and fears
    of those who need me and of those who long to know you.

Paul S. McElroy

~ 289 ~

O Lord my God, my creator and my re-creator,
    My soul longs for you.
Tell me what you are, beyond what I have seen,
    So that I may see clearly what I desire.

St. Anselm

⌒ 290 ⌒

We bring before you, O Lord:
The troubles and perils of people and nations,
The sighing of prisoners and captives,
The sorrows of the bereaved,
The necessities of strangers,
The helplessness of the weak,
The despondency of the weary,
The failing powers of the aged.
O Lord, draw near to each.
For the sake of Jesus Christ our Lord.

St. Anselm

⌒ 291 ⌒

For this reason I kneel before the Father,
    from whom his whole family in heaven
    and on earth derives its name.
I pray that out of his glorious riches he may strengthen you
    with power through his Spirit in your inner being,
    so that Christ may dwell in your hearts through faith.
And I pray that you, being rooted and established in love,
    may have power, together with all the saints,
    to grasp how wide and long and high and deep
    is the love of Christ,
    and to know this love that surpasses knowledge—
    that you may be filled
    to the measure of all the fullness of God.

Ephesians 3:14-19 (NIV)

~ 292 ~

Your love, O Lord, reaches to the heavens,
    your faithfulness to the skies.
Your righteousness is like the mighty mountains,
    your justice like the great deep.
O Lord, you preserve both man and beast.
How priceless is your unfailing love!

Psalm 36:5-7 (NIV)

~ 293 ~

Come to us, O Lord!
Open the eyes of our souls, and show us
        the things which belong to our peace
        and the path of life, that we may see that,
        though all man's inventions and plans come to an end,
        yet thy commandment is exceeding broad—
        broad enough for rich and poor,
        for scholar, tradesman, and laborer;
        for our prosperity in this life,
        and our salvation in the life to come.

Charles Kingsley

~ 294 ~

Lord, I asked you for abundant life
Rich, challenging, full of adventure
And you said Yes.
I asked you for an undisturbable joy
Independent of transitory change
And you said Yes.
I asked you to thread my tears into a song
When I was shattered and torn with grief
And you said Yes.
I asked you to steady me when I staggered—
To hold me when I struggled
To seize me when I resisted
And you said Yes.
I asked you to forgive my vain grasping
My foolish fears, my willful pride
And you said Yes.
I asked you to be my Helper, my Friend
My Light in the darkness
And you said Yes.
I asked you to guide me all my life
With your wisdom, your counsel
Your captivating love
And you said Yes.
Sometimes, Lord
I feel like a spoiled child
Who gets whatever he asks for.
You overwhelm me with joy.
For *you love to say Yes!*

Ruth Harms Calkin

~ 295 ~

Our Father in heaven, I thank thee
    that thou hast led me into the light.
I thank thee for sending the Savior to call me from death to life.
I confess that I was dead in sin before I heard his call,
    but when I heard him, like Lazarus, I arose.
But, O my Father, the grave clothes bind me still.
Old habits that I cannot throw off, old customs that are so much a
    part of my life that I am helpless
    to live the new life that Christ calls me to live.
Give me strength, O Father, to break the bonds;
Give me courage to live a new life in thee;
Give me faith, to believe that with thy help I cannot fail.
And this I ask in the Savior's name
    who has taught me to come to thee.

Author unknown (Taiwan)

~ 296 ~

O God, who by thine almighty Word dost enlighten
    every man that cometh into the world:
Enlighten, we beseech thee,
    the hearts of us thy servants by the glory of thy grace,
That we may ever think such things
    as are worthy and well-pleasing to thy Majesty,
And love thee with a perfect heart.

Alcuin

～ *297* ～

Lord, I haven't accomplished a thing all day.
And, it's been great!
This morning I stood out in the yard.
Just stood,
and looked,
and smelled,
and listened.
A mockingbird sang matins for me.
Roses and peach trees scented my reverie.
And I saw jewels . . . rubies and emeralds and gorgeous things
hanging on the fence, left over from last night's rain.
I squandered half the afternoon with a book,
the other half with a friend.
And then, we went on a picnic.
The kids chortled and cavorted.
I hadn't squished mud through my toes for years!
It's been a delightful, renewing, refreshing day, Lord—
And I give thanks for it.

Jo Carr & Imogene Sorley

～ *298* ～

Open my eyes that I may see wonderful things in your law.

Psalm 119:18 (NIV)

～ 299 ～

For the beauty of the earth,
For the beauty of the sky,
For the love which from our birth
Over and around us lies,
Lord of all, to thee we raise
This our joyful hymn of praise.
For the joy of human love,
Brother, sister, parent, child,
Friends on earth, and friends above,
For all gentle thoughts and mild,
Lord of all, to thee we raise
This our joyful hymn of praise.

Folliott Sandford Pierpoint

～ 300 ～

O sing unto the Lord a new song.
Sing unto the Lord, all the earth.
Sing unto the Lord, bless his name.
Show forth his salvation from day to day.
Declare his glory among the heathen,
his wonders among all people.
For the Lord is great, and greatly to be praised. . . .

Psalm 96:1–4 (KJV)

∼ 301 ∼

. . . Lord, save me.

Matthew 14:30 (KJV)

∼ 302 ∼

Be merciful to me, O God, for men hotly pursue me;
    all day long they press their attack.
My slanderers pursue me all day long;
    many are attacking me in their pride.
When I am afraid, I will trust in you.
In God, whose word I praise, in God I trust; I will not be afraid.
What can mortal man do to me?
All day long they twist my words; they are always plotting to harm me.
They conspire, they lurk, they watch my steps, eager to take my life. . . .
Record my lament; list my tears on your scroll—
    are they not in your record?
Then my enemies will turn back when I call for help.
By this I will know that God is for me.
In God, whose word I praise, in the Lord, whose word I praise—
    in God I trust; I will not be afraid.
What can man do to me?

Psalm 56:1-6, 8-11 (NIV)

∼ 303 ∼

What shall befall us hereafter we know not;
    but to God, who cares for all people,
who will one day reveal the secrets of all hearts,
    we commit ourselves wholly,
    with all who are near and dear to us.

Matthew Parker

～ *304* ～

Shout for joy to the Lord, all the earth.
Worship the Lord with gladness;
    come before him with joyful songs.
Know that the Lord is God.
It is he who made us, and we are his;
    we are his people, the sheep of his pasture.
Enter his gates with thanksgiving and his courts with praise;
    give thanks to him and praise his name.
For the Lord is good and his love endures forever;
    his faithfulness continues through all generations.

Psalm 100 (NIV)

～ *305* ～

Our Father which art in heaven,
Hallowed be thy name.
Thy kingdom come.
Thy will be done in earth, as it is in heaven.
Give us this day our daily bread.
And forgive us our debts, as we forgive our debtors.
And lead us not into temptation, but deliver us from evil:
For thine is the kingdom, and the power, and the glory, for ever.
Amen.

Matthew 6:9b–13 (KJV)

~ *306* ~

Hear my prayer, O Lord, and let my cry come unto thee.
Hide not thy face from me in the day when I am in trouble.
Incline thine ear unto me. In the day when I call answer me speedily.

Psalm 102:1-2 (KJV)

~ *307* ~

Thou knowest, Father, the things of which we are afraid—
 the terror by night, the arrow by day that takes us unawares
 and often finds us without a vital, ready faith.
Help us to remember, O Christ, that thou art victorious . . .
 reigning over all;
That in due time, in thine own good time,
Thou wilt work all things together for good to them that love thee,
 who are called according to thy purpose.
May we find our refuge in that . . . faith,
 and so face the future without fear.
Give to us thy peace, through Jesus Christ, our Lord.

Peter Marshall

~ *308* ~

Hear us, O never-failing light, Lord our God, the fountain of light,
   the light of your angels, principalities, powers,
   and of all intelligent beings;
   who has created the light of your saints.
May our souls be lamps of yours, kindled and illuminated by you.
May they shine and burn with the truth,
   and never go out in darkness and ashes.
May the gloom of sins be cleared away,
   and the light of perpetual faith abide within us.

Mozarabic

~ *309* ~

The Lord is my light and my salvation—
   whom shall I fear?
The Lord is the stronghold of my life—
   of whom shall I be afraid?

Psalm 27:1 (NIV)

～ 310 ～

I asked for Peace—
My sins arose, and bound me close,
I could not find release.

I asked for Truth—
My doubts came in, and with their din
They wearied all my youth.

I asked for Love—
My lovers failed, and griefs assailed
Around, beneath, above.

I asked for thee—
And thou didst come to take me home
Within thy Heart to be.

Digby M. Dolben

～ 311 ～

Praise the Lord, O my soul;
   all my inmost being, praise his holy name.
Praise the Lord, O my soul, and forget not all his benefits—
   who forgives all your sins and heals all your diseases,
   who redeems your life from the pit
   and crowns you with love and compassion,
   who satisfies your desires with good things
   so that your youth is renewed like the eagle's.

Psalm 103:1-5 (NIV)

~ 312 ~

Nothing, O Lord, is more like your holy nature
    than the mind that is settled in quietness.
You have called us into that quietness and peace
    from out of the turmoils of this world—
    as it were, from out of storms into a haven.
It is a peace the world cannot give,
    and that surpasses all human capacity.
Grant now, O most merciful Father, that,
    through your overwhelming goodness,
    our minds may yield themselves
    in obedience to you without striving;
And that they may quietly rise into your sovereign rest.
May nothing disturb or disquiet us here.
Rather, let us be calm and quiet in your peace.

A Book of Christian Prayers

~ 313 ~

Listen, Lord, a mother's praying low and quiet.
Listen, please.
Listen what her tears are saying.
See her heart upon its knees.
Lift the load from her bowed shoulders
Till she sees and understands.
You, who hold the worlds together,
Hold her problems in your hands.

Ruth Bell Graham

~ 314 ~

And the children of Isreal said unto the Lord,
"We have sinned:
  do thou unto us whatsoever seemeth good unto thee;
  deliver us only, we pray thee, this day."

Judges 10:15 (KJV)

~ 315 ~

You are my hiding place;
you will protect me from trouble
and surround me with songs of deliverance.

Psalm 32:7 (NIV)

~ *316* ~

Heal me, O Lord, and I will be healed;
save me and I will be saved,
for you are the one I praise. . . .

Jeremiah 17:14 (NIV)

~ *317* ~

O loving and tender Father in heaven, we confess before you,
in sorrow, how hard and unsympathetic are our hearts;
How often we have sinned against our neighbors
by want of compassion and tenderness;
How often we have felt no true pity for their trials and sorrows,
and have neglected to comfort, help, and visit them.
O Father, forgive this our sin, and lay it not to our charge.
Give us grace ever to alleviate the crosses and difficulties
of those around us, and never to add to them;
Teach us to be consolers in sorrow, to take thought for the stranger,
the widow, and the orphan;
Let our charity show itself not in words only, but in deed and truth.
Teach us to judge as you do, with forbearance,
with much pity and indulgence;
And help us to avoid all unloving judgment of others.

Johann Arndt

～ 318 ～

. . . God, have mercy on me, a sinner.

Luke 18:13 (NIV)

～ 319 ～

O my God, how can we find pleasure in doing what offends thee?
Give me the heart of an angel that I may love thee
    and cause thee to be loved.
Make use of me to kindle the fire of thy love in all hearts.

Abbe Lasausse

～ 320 ～

. . . Father, I have sinned against heaven, and before thee,
    and am no more worthy to be called thy son.
Make me as one of thy hired servants.

Luke 15:18-19 (KJV)

~ *321* ~

Give us courage, gaiety and the quiet mind.
Spare us to our friends, soften to us our enemies.
Bless us, if it may be, in all our innocent endeavors.
If it may not, give us the strength to encounter that which is to come,
    that we be brave in peril, constant in tribulation,
    temperate in wrath,
      and in all changes of fortune and down to the gates of death,
    loyal and loving one to another.

Robert Louis Stevenson

~ *322* ~

O God of surpassing goodness,
    whom the round world with one voice
    does praise for your sweet kindness;
We pray you to remove from us all error,
    that so we may perform your will.
Through Jesus Christ our Lord.

Sarum Breviary

~ 323 ~

I will proclaim the name of the Lord.
Oh, praise the greatness of our God!
He is the Rock, his works are perfect,
and all his ways are just.
A faithful God who does no wrong,
upright and just is he.

Deuteronomy 32:3-4 (KJV)

~ 324 ~

. . . My heart rejoices in the Lord; . . .
There is no one holy like the Lord,
there is no one besides you;
there is no Rock like our God.

The Lord sends poverty and wealth;
he humbles and he exalts.
He raises the poor from the dust
and lifts the needy from the ash heap;
he seats them with princes
and has them inherit a throne of honor. . . .

I Samuel 2:1-2, 7-8 (NIV)

~ *325* ~

God of our life,
There are days when the burdens we carry
    chafe our shoulders and weigh us down;
When the road seems dreary and endless,
    the skies grey and threatening;
When our lives have no music in them,
    and our hearts are lonely,
    and our souls have lost their courage.
Flood the path with light, we beseech thee.
Turn our eyes to where the skies are full of promise.
Tune our hearts to brave music.
Give us the sense of comradeship with heroes
    and saints of every age
    and so quicken our spirits
    that we may be able to encourage the souls
    of all who journey with us on the road to life.
To thy honor and glory.

St. Augustine

~ *326* ~

Keep me as the apple of your eye;
hide me in the shadow of your wings.

Psalm 17:8 (NIV)

～ 327 ～

My God, grant that I may serve thee with a pure heart;
  that I may seek only thy glory.
Thou wilt come to my help in all my needs,
  because thou art my Father.

Abbe Lasausse

～ 328 ～

Lord, you have assigned me my portion and my cup;
  you have made my lot secure.
The boundary lines have fallen for me in pleasant places;
  surely I have a delightful inheritance.
I will praise the Lord, who counsels me;
  even at night my heart instructs me.
I have set the Lord always before me.
Because he is at my right hand, I will not be shaken.
You have made known to me the path of life;
  you will fill me with joy in your presence,
  with eternal pleasures at your right hand.

Psalm 16:5-8, 11 (NIV)

~ *329* ~

Lord, give me this soul!
I have waked for it when I should have slept.
I have yearned over it, and I have wept,
Til in my own mind the thought of it held sway
All through the night and day.

Lord, give me this soul!
If I might only lift its broken strands,
To lay them gently in thy loving hands—
If I might know it had found peace in thee,
What rest, what peace to me!

Thou wilt give me this soul!
Else why the joy, the grief, the doubt, the pain
The thought perpetual, the one refrain,
The ceaseless longing that upon thy breast
The tempest-tossed may rest?
Dear Lord, give me this soul!

An Anonymous Mother

~ *330* ~

Now may the Lord of peace himself give you peace at all times
and in every way.
The Lord be with all of you.

II Thessalonians 3:16 (NIV)

~ *331* ~

On building a wall:
I pray thee, Lord, to make my faith as firmly established
    as a house built upon a rock,
        so that neither rain, flood nor wind can ever destroy it.
On pruning a tree:
I pray thee, Lord, to purge me and take away
    my selfishness and sinful thoughts,
        that I may bring forth more fruits of the Spirit.
On tending sheep:
I pray thee, Lord, to protect me from evil and keep me from want,
    daily carrying me in thine arms like a lamb.
On winnowing grain:
I pray thee, Lord, to winnow away the chaff from my heart
    and make it like the true wheat, fit to be garnered in thy barn.
On sowing seed:
I pray thee, Lord, to sow the good seed of virtue in my heart,
    letting it grow by day and night and bring forth a hundredfold.
On writing a book:
I pray thee, Lord, by the precious blood of Jesus,
    to pay my debt of sin and write my name in heaven,
        making me free in body and soul.
On planing wood:
I pray thee, Lord, to make me smooth and straight,
    fit to be a useful vessel, pleasing to the Lord.
On drawing water:
I pray thee, Lord, to give living water to quench my thirst,
    and wash away the stains from my heart.

Prayer of Chinese Christian men

~ *332* ~

O God, who hast in thy love kept me vigorously and joyfully at work
    in days gone by, and dost now send me joyful and contented
    into silence and inactivity;
Grant me to find happiness in thee in all my solitary and quiet hours.
In thy strength, O God, I bid farewell to all.
The past thou knowest: I leave it at thy feet.
Grant me grace to respond to thy divine call,
    to leave all that is dear on earth, and go alone to thee.
Behold, I come quickly, saith the Lord.
Come, Lord Jesus.

Prayer of an Indian priest in old age

~ *333* ~

. . . Father, into thy hands, I commend my spirit.

Luke 23:46 (KJV)

~ *334* ~

Lord God . . .
As I sit here silently with my friend of many years
Please let her know how deeply I care.
How achingly I long to comfort her grief-stupored heart.
Make me just now a gentle transmitter of your calming peace.
Her anguish is too deep for words—at least my words, Lord.
She needs the solace of *your* words
Whispered assuringly to her waiting heart.
In her new-born pain you alone can sustain her.
In the long, tedious climb from rock-bottom
You alone can stabilize her.

Without you there is only despair
But praise upon praise
She is never without you!

Ruth Harms Calkin

~ *335* ~

Christ within me is my glory.
The brightness of his presence wipes out all darkness,
and I am filled with life and light.

Charles Fillmore

~ 336 ~

It comes as a clear admonition, Lord—"Judge not."
But I do judge. . . . And why, Lord?
What is this bias that causes me to classify . . . and pigeonhole people?
And then accept without challenge the automatic condemnation
    that my prejudice metes out?
What is this self-conceit that makes me consider myself
    wise enough . . . or *good* enough to judge?
I know the admonition, Lord. But I forget.
I shift my mind to automatic,
    and it goes right on making oversimplified generalizations . . .
    which I accept without question.
Ah, Lord—forgive.

Jo Carr & Imogene Sorley

~ 337 ~

My God, I do not desire riches, or honors, or pleasures in this world.
I do not desire the esteem of creatures, or life, or health.
I desire nothing of earth.
I desire only the accomplishment of thy will.

Abbe Lasausse

∼ 338 ∼

. . . O my Father, if it be possible,
let this cup pass from me:
nevertheless, not as I will,
but as thou wilt.

Matthew 26:39 (KJV)

∼ 339 ∼

Visit me not, O my loving Lord—if it be not wrong so to pray—
visit me not with those trying visitations
which saints alone can bear!
Pity my weakness,
and lead me heavenwards in a safe and tranquil course.
Still I leave all in your hands—
only, if you shall bring heavier trials on me,
give me more grace,
Flood me with the fullness of your strength and consolation.

John Henry Newman

∼ 340 ∼

O Lord,
I do not pray for tasks equal to my strength:
I ask for strength equal to my tasks.

Phillips Brooks

∼ 341 ∼

The Lord is my shepherd; I shall not want.
He maketh me to lie down in green pastures:
    he leadeth me beside the still waters.
He restoreth my soul:
    he leadeth me in the paths of righteousness for his name's sake.
Yea, though I walk through the valley of the shadow of death,
    I will fear no evil: for thou art with me;
    thy rod and thy staff they comfort me.
Thou preparest a table before me in the presence of mine enemies:
    thou anointest my head with oil, my cup runneth over.
Surely goodness and mercy shall follow me all the days of my life;
    and I will dwell in the house of the Lord for ever.

Psalm 23 (KJV)

∼ 342 ∼

Be, Lord, within me to strengthen me,
    without me to preserve,
    over me to shelter,
    beneath me to support,
    before me to direct,
    behind me to bring back,
    round about me to fortify.

Lancelot Andrewes

~ 343 ~

Grant, O merciful God, that with malice toward none,
    with charity to all,
    with firmness in the right as you give us to see the right,
    we may strive to finish the work we are in;
    to bind up the nation's wounds;
    to care for him who shall have borne the battle
    and for his widow and his orphan;
    to do all which may achieve and cherish a just and lasting peace
    among ourselves and with all nations.

Abraham Lincoln

~ 344 ~

O Lord, renew our spirits and draw our hearts unto thyself,
    that our work may not be to us a burden, but a delight.
And give us such a mighty love to thee
    as may sweeten our obedience.
O let us not serve thee with the spirit of bondage as slaves,
    but with cheerfulness and gladness,
    delighting ourselves in thee and rejoicing in thy work.

Benjamin Jenks

~ *345* ~

O God . . . we have been slow to the calls of affection,
heedless of the duties,
hard under the sorrows, which are your gracious discipline;
Yet are oppressed with cares you lay not on us,
with ease you do not permit, and wants you will never bless.
Visit us with the wrestlings of your Spirit: and lay on us the cross,
if we may but grow into the holiness of Christ.

James Martineau

~ *346* ~

I ask pardon, O my amiable Savior,
because I have so often pierced thy heart by sin.
Be merciful.
Give me wisdom that it may enlighten my mind
and wound my heart with love.

Abbe Lasausse

~ *347* ~

The Lord our God be with us, as he was with our fathers.
Let him not leave us, nor forsake us.
That he may incline our hearts unto him,
    to walk in all his ways, and to keep his commandments,
    and his statutes, and his judgments,
    which he commanded our fathers.

I Kings 8:57-58 (KJV)

~ *348* ~

Eternal God, who hast taught us by thy holy word
    that our bodies are temples of thy Spirit,
    keep us, we most humbly beseech thee,
    temperate and holy in thought, word, and deed,
    that at the last, with all the pure in heart,
    we may see thee, and be made like unto thee
    in thy heavenly kingdom.

Bishop Brook Foss Westcott

~ *349* ~

. . . Naked came I out of my mother's womb,
and naked shall I return thither;
The Lord gave, and the Lord hath taken away;
blessed be the name of the Lord.

Job 1:21 (KJV)

~ *350* ~

Help us, O Holy Spirit, giver of life and love,
to be always so mindful of the love from whence we came,
that we may learn more and more the love to which we go;
and in this love abounding, daily abide.

E. Milner-White

~ *351* ~

O my God, I return thee my heart.
It belongs to thee.
Grant that it may never be attached to things of earth;
that I may find no pleasure but in thee.

Abbe Lasausse

~ *352* ~

Living or dying, Lord, I would be yours.
Keep me your own forever,
and draw me day by day nearer to yourself,
Until I be wholly filled with your love,
and fitted to behold you, face to face.

Edward Bouverie Pusey

~ *353* ~

. . . The harvest truly is plenteous,
but the laborers are few.
Pray ye therefore the Lord of the harvest,
that he will send forth laborers into his harvest.

Matthew 9:37–38 (KJV)

~ *354* ~

O Lord . . . may we learn to love you whom we have not seen,
by loving our brothers and sisters whom we have seen.
Teach us, O heavenly Father, the love by which you have loved us.
Fashion us, O blessed Lord, after your own example of love.
Shed abroad, O Holy Spirit of love, the love of God . . . in our hearts.

Henry Alford

~ *355* ~

O Holy Spirit, descend plentifully into my heart.
Enlighten the dark corners of this neglected dwelling
and scatter there thy cheerful beams.

St. Augustine

∼ 356 ∼

O Lord Jesus Christ, exalt me with thee
    so to know the mystery of life that I may use the earthly
    as the appointed expression and type of the heavenly;
And by using to thy grace the natural body,
I may be fit to be exalted
    to the use of the spiritual body.

Charles Kingsley

∼ 357 ∼

Lord of my Being, I would be disentangled from
    the servitude and vicissitudes of the formed world.
I would do all thou wouldst have me do.
I would be "in the world but not of it."
I would dwell in the gloriousness
    of thine omnipresent companionship.
I would always be still enough to hear thy voice
    instead of the confusion and clamor of senses.
I would know and not assume.
I would truly live and not exist.

Myrtle Fillmore

~ 358 ~

Use me, God, in thy great harvest field,
Which stretcheth far and wide like a wide sea;
The gatherers are so few;
I fear the precious yield will suffer loss.
Oh, find a place for me!
A place where best the strength I have will tell:
It may be one the older toilers shun;
Be it a wide or narrow place, 'tis well
So that the work it holds be only done.

Christina Rossetti

~ 359 ~

O Lord, let us not live to be useless.
For Christ's sake. Amen.

John Wesley

～ 360 ～

Lord, who has given all for us:
help us to give all for thee.

G. W. Briggs

～ 361 ～

O God, who dividest day from night,
give us hearts and minds unshadowed by the gloom of evil,
That we may think continually upon things
that are good and wholesome,
And be always pleasing in thy sight.

Gelasian Sacramentary

～ 362 ～

O Lord, forgive what I have been,
Sanctify what I am,
And order what I shall be.

Author unknown

~ *363* ~

O Lord, we beseech thee to deliver us
  from the fear of the unknown future;
  from fear of failure; from fear of poverty;
  from fear of bereavement;
  from fear of loneliness; from fear of sickness and pain;
  from fear of fear of age; and from fear of death.
Help us, O Father, by thy grace to love and fear thee only,
  fill our hearts with cheerful courage and loving trust in thee;
  through our Lord and Master Jesus Christ.

Akuna Ibain, Nigeria

~ *364* ~

O our God, who opens your hand,
  and fills all things living with plenteousness,
  unto you we commit all those who are dear to us.
Watch over them, we beg of you, and provide all things needful
  for their souls and bodies, from this time forth for evermore.
Through Jesus Christ our Lord.

St. Nerses

～ 365 ～

Peace be in thy home
And in thy heart,
Or if thou roam
Earth's highways wide,
The Lord be at thy side,
To bless and guide.

Author unknown

～ Acknowledgments ～

A careful effort has been made to trace the ownership of poems used in this collection and give proper acknowledgment. We will gladly correct any errors or omissions in future editions, provided that written notification is made to the publisher: Ottenheimer Publishers, Inc., 5 Park Center Court, Owings Mills, Maryland, 21117.

A Book of Christian Prayers: from *Prayers Across the Centuries*, Vinita Hampton Wright, Ed. © 1993 by Harold Shaw Publishers. Used by permission of Harold Shaw Publishers.

Alcuin: from *The Prayer Manual*, Frederick B. Macnutt, Compiler. © 1961 A.R. Mowbray & Co. Limited. Used by permission of Cassell PLC.

Alford, Henry: from *Prayers Across the Centuries*, Vinita Hampton Wright, Ed. © 1993 by Harold Shaw Publishers. Used by permission of Harold Shaw Publishers.

Alfred the Great: from *Prayers Across the Centuries*, Vinita Hampton Wright, Ed. © 1993 by Harold Shaw Publishers. Used by permission of Harold Shaw Publishers.

Allen, Andrew Harding: from *Words of Wisdom, Words of Praise*. Blue Mountain Press, Boulder, CO.: 1979. © 1979 Continental Publications and Sandpiper Studios, Inc. Reprinted with permission of Continental Publications.

Ambrose, Saint: from Prayers Across the Centuries, Vinita Hampton Wright, Ed. © 1993 by Harold Shaw Publishers. Used by permission of Harold Shaw Publishers.

Andrewes, Lancelot: from *The Prayer Manual*, Frederick B. Macnutt, Compiler. © 1961 A.R. Mowbray & Co. Limited. Used by permission of Cassell PLC.

Anonymous Mother and Anonymous Teacher: from *Wings of Joy*, by Joan Winmill Brown. Reprinted by permission of Fleming H. Revell Company, a division of Baker Book House. © 1977 Joan Winmill Brown.

Anselm, Saint (No. 229): from *The Prayer Manual*, Frederick B. Macnutt, Compiler. © 1961 A.R. Mowbray & Co. Limited. Used by permission of Cassell PLC.

Anselm, Saint (Nos. 289 and 290): from *Prayers Across the Centuries*, Vinita Hampton Wright, Ed. © 1993 by Harold Shaw Publishers. Used by permission of Harold Shaw Publishers.

Arndt, Johann: from *Prayers Across the Centuries*, Vinita Hampton Wright, Ed. © 1993 by Harold Shaw Publishers. Used by permission of Harold Shaw Publishers.

Benet, Stephen Vincent: from *Words of Wisdom*, Words of Praise. Blue Mountain Press, Boulder, CO.: 1979. © 1979 Continental Publications and Sandpiper Studios, Inc. Used by permission of Blue Mountain Press, Inc.

Bernardin, Joseph L.: Reprinted from *The Journalist's Prayer Book* by Alfred P. Klauser and John De Mott, copyright © 1987 Augsburg Publishing House. Used by permission of Augsburg Fortress.

Bonhoeffer, Dietrich: from *Prayers Across the Centuries*, Vinita Hampton Wright, Ed. © 1993 by Harold Shaw Publishers. Used by permission of Harold Shaw Publishers.

Book of Christian Prayers: from *Prayers Across the Centuries*, Vinita Hampton Wright, Ed. © 1993 by Harold Shaw Publishers. Used by permission of Harold Shaw Publishers.

Book of Common Prayer: from *Prayers Across the Centuries*, Vinita Hampton Wright, Ed. © 1993 by Harold Shaw Publishers. Used by permission of Harold Shaw Publishers.

Booth, William: from *Prayers Across the Centuries*, Vinita Hampton Wright, Ed. © 1993 by Harold Shaw Publishers. Used by permission of Harold Shaw Publishers.

Briggs, G. W.: from *The Prayer Manual*, Frederick B. Macnutt, Compiler. © 1961 A.R. Mowbray & Co. Limited. Used by permission of Cassell PLC.

Bright, William: from *The Prayer Manual*, Frederick B. Macnutt, Compiler. © 1961 A.R. Mowbray & Co. Limited. Used by permission of Cassell PLC.

Brooks, Phillips: from *The Prayer Manual*, Frederick B. Macnutt, Compiler. © 1961 A.R. Mowbray & Co. Limited. Used by permission of Cassell PLC.

Calkin, Ruth Harms: from *Lord, You Love to Say Yes*, by Ruth Harms Calkin. © 1976. Used by permission of Tyndale House Publishers, Inc. All rights reserved.

Carr, Jo and Imogene Sorley: from *Plum Jelly and Stained Glass & Other Prayers* by Jo Carr and Imogene Sorley. Copyright © 1973 by Abingdon Press. Used by permission.

Carter, Thomas Thellusson: from *Prayers Across the Centuries*, Vinita Hampton Wright, Ed. © 1993 by Harold Shaw Publishers. Used by permission of Harold Shaw Publishers.

Chinese Christian Men and Women: from *Morning, Noon and Night*, Rev. John Carden, Ed. Used by permission of the Church Missionary Society.

Collins, Bavid B.: Reprinted from *The Journalist's Prayer Book* by Alfred P. Klauser and John De Mott. Copyright © 1987 Augsburg Publishing House. Used by permission of Augsburg Fortress.

Contemporary Prayers for Public Worship, Caryl Micklem, Ed. SCM Press, 1967. Used by permission of SCM Press Ltd.

Lasausse, The Abbe: from *A Happy Year; or the Year Sanctified by Meditating on the Maxims and Sayings of the Saints*. Benziger Brothers, Printers to the Holy Apostolic See, 1890.

Laud, Archbishop: from *The Prayer Manual*, Frederick B. Macnutt, Compiler. © 1961 A.R. Mowbray & Co. Limited. Used by permission of Cassell PLC.

Leofric, Bishop of Exeter: from *Prayers Across the Centuries*, Vinita Hampton Wright, Ed. © 1993 by Harold Shaw Publishers. Used by permission of Harold Shaw Publishers.

Leonine Sacramentary (No. 219): from *The Prayer Manual*, Frederick B. Macnutt, Compiler. © 1961 A.R. Mowbray & Co. Limited. Used by permission of Cassell PLC.

Leonine Sacramentary (No. 80): from *Prayers Across the Centuries*, Vinita Hampton Wright, Ed. © 1993 by Harold Shaw Publishers. Used by permission of Harold Shaw Publishers.

Lincoln, Abraham: from *Prayers Across the Centuries*, Vinita Hampton Wright, Ed. © 1993 by Harold Shaw Publishers. Used by permission of Harold Shaw Publishers.

Luther, Martin: from *Prayers Across the Centuries*, Vinita Hampton Wright, Ed. © 1993 by Harold Shaw Publishers. Used by permission of Harold Shaw Publishers.

Macnutt, Frederick B.: from *The Prayer Manual*, Frederick B. Macnutt, Compiler. © 1961 A.R. Mowbray & Co. Limited. Used by permission of Cassell PLC.

Mark, Saint: from *Prayers Across the Centuries*, Vinita Hampton Wright, Ed. © 1993 by Harold Shaw Publishers. Used by permission of Harold Shaw Publishers.

Marshall, Peter (Nos. 22, 157, and 198): from *Prayers Across the Centuries*, Vinita Hampton Wright, Ed. © 1993 by Harold Shaw Publishers. Used by permission of Harold Shaw Publishers.

Marshall, Peter (Nos. 25, 94, and 307): from *The Prayers of Peter Marshall*, Catherine Marshall, Ed. © 1949, 1950, 1951, 1954 by Catherine Marshall. Used by permission of Chosen Books, Inc., a division of Baker Book House.

Martineau, James: from *Prayers Across the Centuries*, Vinita Hampton Wright, Ed. © 1993 by Harold Shaw Publishers. Used by permission of Harold Shaw Publishers.

Martyn, Henry: from *Prayers Across the Centuries*, Vinita Hampton Wright, Ed. © 1993 by Harold Shaw Publishers. Used by permission of Harold Shaw Publishers.

McElroy, Paul S.: from *Prayers for Inner Strength*, John Beilenson, Comp. © 1986 Peter Pauper Press. White Plains, NY. Used by permission of Peter Pauper Press.

Mechthild of Mageburg, Saint: from *Prayers Across the Centuries*, Vinita Hampton Wright, Ed. © 1993 by Harold Shaw Publishers. Used by permission of Harold Shaw Publishers.

Melancthon, Philip: from *Prayers Across the Centuries*, Vinita Hampton Wright, Ed. © 1993 by Harold Shaw Publishers. Used by permission of Harold Shaw Publishers.

Milner-White, E.: from *The Prayer Manual*, Frederick B. Macnutt, Compiler. © 1961 A.R. Mowbray & Co. Limited. Used by permission of Cassell PLC.

Moody, Dwight L.: from *The Prayer Manual*, Frederick B. Macnutt, Compiler. © 1961 A.R. Mowbray & Co. Limited. Used by permission of Cassell PLC.

Mother Teresa of Calcutta: from *Prayers Across the Centuries*, Vinita Hampton Wright, Ed. © 1993 by Harold Shaw Publishers. Used by permission of Harold Shaw Publishers.

Mozarabic (No. 98): from *The Prayer Manual*, Frederick B. Macnutt, Compiler. © 1961 A.R. Mowbray & Co. Limited. Used by permission of Cassell PLC.

Mozarabic (Nos. 88 and 308): from *Prayers Across the Centuries*, Vinita Hampton Wright, Ed. © 1993 by Harold Shaw Publishers. Used by permission of Harold Shaw Publishers.

Nerses, Saint: from *Prayers Across the Centuries*, Vinita Hampton Wright, Ed. © 1993 by Harold Shaw Publishers. Used by permission of Harold Shaw Publishers.

Newman, John Henry: from *Prayers Across the Centuries*, Vinita Hampton Wright, Ed. © 1993 by Harold Shaw Publishers. Used by permission of Harold Shaw Publishers.

Niebuhr, Reinhold: from *Justice and Mercy* by Reinhold Niebuhr, edited by Ursula M. Niebuhr. © 1974 Ursula M. Niebuhr. Used by permission of Westminster John Knox Press.

Parker, Matthew: from *Prayers Across the Centuries*, Vinita Hampton Wright, Ed. © 1993 by Harold Shaw Publishers. Used by permission of Harold Shaw Publishers.

Pascal, Blaise: from *Prayers Across the Centuries*, Vinita Hampton Wright, Ed. © 1993 by Harold Shaw Publishers. Used by permission of Harold Shaw Publishers.

Paterson, Sir Alexander: from *The Prayer Manual*, Frederick B. Macnutt, Compiler. © 1961 A.R. Mowbray & Co. Limited. Used by permission of Cassell PLC.

Paterson, Evangeline: from *Prayers Across the Centuries*, Vinita Hampton Wright, Ed. © 1993 by Harold Shaw Publishers. Used by permission of Harold Shaw Publishers.

Patrick, Saint: from *The Prayer Manual*, Frederick B. Macnutt, Compiler. © 1961 A.R. Mowbray & Co. Limited. Used by permission of Cassell PLC.

Pierpoint, Folliott Sandford: from *Prayers Across the Centuries*, Vinita Hampton Wright, Ed. © 1993 by Harold Shaw Publishers. Used by permission of Harold Shaw Publishers.

Popish, Minnie Boyd: from *The Symphony of Life from the Salesian Collection*, Sara Tarascio, Comp. New Rochelle, NY: 1994. Used by permission of the author.

Prayerbook: from *Prayers Across the Centuries*, Vinita Hampton Wright, Ed. © 1993 by Harold Shaw Publishers. Used by permission of Harold Shaw Publishers.

Punjabi Christian: from *Morning, Noon and Night*, Rev. John Carden, Ed. Used by permission of the Church Missionary Society.

Pusey, Edward Bouverie (Nos. 85, 228, and 352): from *Prayers Across the Centuries*, Vinita Hampton Wright, Ed. © 1993 by Harold Shaw Publishers. Used by permission of Harold Shaw Publishers.

Pusey, Edward Bouverie (No. 281): from *Prayers for Inner Strength*, John Beilenson, Comp. © 1986 Peter Pauper Press. White Plains, NY. Used by permission of Peter Pauper Press.

Ridley, Bishop: from *The Prayer Manual*, Frederick B. Macnutt, Compiler. © 1961 A.R. Mowbray & Co. Limited. Used by permission of Cassell PLC.

Rossetti, Christina (Nos. 24, 71, 226, and 271): from *Prayers Across the Centuries*, Vinita Hampton Wright, Ed. © 1993 by Harold Shaw Publishers. Used by permission of Harold Shaw Publishers.

Rossetti, Christina (No. 191): from *Prayers for Inner Strength*, John Beilenson, Comp. © 1986 Peter Pauper Press. White Plains, NY. Used by permission of Peter Pauper Press.

Rossetti, Christina (Nos. 174, 233, and 358): from *Wings of Joy*, by Joan Winmill Brown. Reprinted by permission of Fleming H. Revell Company, a division of Baker Book House. © 1977 Joan Winmill Brown.

Sarum Breviary (No. 153): from *The Prayer Manual*, Frederick B. Macnutt, Compiler. © 1961 A.R. Mowbray & Co. Limited. Used by permission of Cassell PLC.

Sarum Breviary (Nos. 67, 181, 279, and 322): from *Prayers Across the Centuries*, Vinita Hampton Wright, Ed. © 1993 by Harold Shaw Publishers. Used by permission of Harold Shaw Publishers.

Sarum Primer: from *The Prayer Manual*, Frederick B. Macnutt, Compiler. © 1961 A.R. Mowbray & Co. Limited. Used by permission of Cassell PLC.

Scripture quotations marked (KJV) are taken from the *Holy Bible*, King James Version.

Snowden, Rita: from *Prayers for the Family*. © 1970 Rita F. Snowden. Reprinted with permission of HarperCollins Publishers.

Socrates: from *Words of Wisdom, Words of Praise*. Blue Mountain Press, Boulder, Co.: 1979. © 1979 Continental Publications and Sandpiper Studios, Inc. Used by permission of Blue Mountain Press.

Solzhenitsyn, Aleksandr: from *Prayers Across the Centuries*, Vinita Hampton Wright, Ed. © 1993 by Harold Shaw Publishers. Used by permission of Harold Shaw Publishers.

Spencer, Malcolm: from *The Prayer Manual*, Frederick B. Macnutt, Compiler. © 1961 A.R. Mowbray & Co. Limited. Used by permission of Cassell PLC.

Stevenson, Robert Louis: from *Prayers for Inner Strength*, John Beilenson, Comp. © 1986 Peter Pauper Press. White Plains, NY. Used by permission of Peter Pauper Press.

Syrian Jacobites: from *Prayers Across the Centuries*, Vinita Hampton Wright, Ed. © 1993 by Harold Shaw Publishers. Used by permission of Harold Shaw Publishers.

Tait, Archibald Campbell: from *Prayers Across the Centuries*, Vinita Hampton Wright, Ed. © 1993 by Harold Shaw Publishers. Used by permission of Harold Shaw Publishers.

Tant, Nancy (No. 257): from *The Symphony of Life from the Salesian Collection*, Sara Tarascio, Comp. New Rochelle, NY: 1994. Used by permission of the author.

Tant, Nancy (Nos. 23 and 262): used by permission of the author.

Taylor, Jeremy (No. 120): from *Prayers Across the Centuries*, Vinita Hampton Wright, Ed. © 1993 by Harold Shaw Publishers. Used by permission of Harold Shaw Publishers.

Taylor, Jeremy (No. 152): from *The Prayer Manual*, Frederick B. Macnutt, Compiler. © 1961 A.R. Mowbray & Co. Limited. Used by permission of Cassell PLC.

Temple, William: from *The Prayer Manual*, Frederick B. Macnutt, Compiler. © 1961 A.R. Mowbray & Co. Limited. Used by permission of Cassell PLC.

Tersteegen, Gerhard: from *Prayers Across the Centuries*, Vinita Hampton Wright, Ed. © 1993 by Harold Shaw Publishers. Used by permission of Harold Shaw Publishers.

Theel, Albert N.: from *The Symphony of Life from the Salesian Collection*, Sara Tarascio, Comp. New Rochelle, NY: 1994. Used by permission of the author.